C000282849

THE SHORT AND EXCRUCIATINGLY EMBARRASSING REIGN OF CAPTAIN ABBOTT

DANIEL BOUD

Andrew P Street is an Adelaide-built, Sydney-based journalist, editor, columnist and failed indie rock star responsible for 'View from the Street' in the digital edition of *The Sydney Morning Herald*. Over the last two decades he's been published internationally in *Time Out, Rolling Stone, NME, The Guardian, GQ* and *Elle*, as well as pretty much every newspaper, magazine and website in Australia with a freelance budget. This is his first book.

THE SHORT AND EXCRUCIATINGLY EMBARRASSING REIGN OF CAPTAIN ABBOTT

ANDREW P STREET

ALLEN&UNWIN
SYDNEY • MELBOURNE • AUCKLAND • LONDON

First published in 2015

Copyright © Andrew P Street 2015

All rights reserved. No part of this book may be reproduced or transmitted in
any form or by any means, electronic or mechanical, including photocopying,
recording or by any information storage and retrieval system, without prior
permission in writing from the publisher. The Australian *Copyright Act 1968*
(the Act) allows a maximum of one chapter or 10 per cent of this book, whichever
is the greater, to be photocopied by any educational institution for its educational
purposes provided that the educational institution (or body that administers it) has
given a remuneration notice to the Copyright Agency (Australia) under the Act.

Allen & Unwin
83 Alexander Street
Crows Nest NSW 2065
Australia
Phone: (61 2) 8425 0100
Email: info@allenandunwin.com
Web: www.allenandunwin.com

Cataloguing-in-Publication details are available
from the National Library of Australia
www.trove.nla.gov.au

ISBN 978 1 76029 054 2

Set in 12/17 pt Adobe Caslon by Midland Typesetters, Australia

Printed and bound in Australia by Griffin Press

10 9 8 7 6 5 4 3 2 1

MIX
Paper from
responsible sources
FSC® C009448
www.fsc.org

The paper in this book is FSC certified.
FSC promotes environmentally responsible,
socially beneficial and economically viable
management of the world's forests.

Charles Rawlings-Way
2015

CONTENTS

Introduction Australia, Stop Hitting Yourself   1

1 The Gathering Storm   9

2 Meet the Motley Crew   29

3 Mandate, Mandate, Mandate!   43

4 The Right to Be a Bigot   53

5 For Those Who've Come Across the Seas . . .   69

6 Classified On-Water Matters   79

7 Putting the Coal into Coalition   91

8 No Cuts to Health   107

9 Not Your Average Jo(k)e   121

10 Meet the New Senate!   137

11 Someone's Getting a Shirtfrontin'   151

12 We All Live in a Competitively Evaluated
    Submarine   163

13 The Terrible, Horrible, No Good, Very Bad
    Spill Motion   177

14 Good Government Starts Today   187

15 I'm a Fixer   207

16 Who's Afraid of Human Rights?   223
17 The Hunt for Team Australia   237
18 Everywhere with Helicopter   247
19 Whither Labor?   257
20 Abandon Ship!   267

Epilogue   Is This the Best We Can Do?   281
Acknowledgement   Or Who's to Blame for this Book   291

INTRODUCTION
AUSTRALIA, STOP HITTING YOURSELF

In which your humble narrator explains why he stowed away aboard this scurvy vessel in the first place.

'Democracy' is a term whose origins lie in two shorter words: the Greek *demos*, meaning 'citizen of the state', and the Old Norse word *acraser*, meaning 'full of cracks'. This is why it's universally understood as meaning 'rule by horribly broken people'.

In that spirit, friends, welcome to a snarky treatise on Australian politics and the short, strange, and embarrassing rule of one Anthony John Abbott, the nation's twenty-eighth, and arguably most foolish, prime minister.

There's no way to sugar-coat it: the politics consumers of Australia have been through some infuriatingly silly times since 2013, and this book is an attempt to contextuali'   'd times in the hope that future generations will learn n them happen again. It's possibly a vain hope, of cou

Australia's not great with history—not least because so much of it is based on invasion, murder and bad decisions leading to often-bloody consequences.

Indeed, for a country whose national humour is deeply, fiercely sarcastic, Australia's surprisingly bad with irony. Perhaps it's because everything about the place reeks of the stuff.

Our national hero is an anti-authoritarian Irish bushranger who defied a corrupt regime of powerful commercial interests and an easily bought justice system to fight against the destructive influences of poverty and discrimination. Our nation-defining military operation was a doomed and bungled beach assault followed by slinking away under cover of darkness, on the orders of an imperial regime that regarded Australians as completely expendable.

And at every sporting event our leaden national anthem is blasted out to the world even as our immigration policies put the lie to the noble declaration trumpeted in the notorious second verse: 'For those who've come across the seas / We've boundless plains to share.' These are the boundless plains that were, as everyone around the world is acutely aware, stolen by a bunch of criminals and foreign interlopers lobbing in on boats. In 2015 such landings were illegal and immoral; in 1788 they represented the proud birth of our plucky nation. Even the overused phrase 'the lucky country', which has functioned as Australia's unofficial motto since Donald Horne's book of the same name was published in 1964, means the exact opposite of what it appears to convey. Unlike the unambiguously bang-on title of the book you're holding now,[1] Horne's was intended as a wry commentary on the nation, not a celebration of our indisputable good fortune—a fact he made clear at the beginning of the final chapter:

> Australia is a lucky country run mainly by second-rate people who share its luck. It lives on other people's ideas, and, although its ordinary people are adaptable, most of its leaders (in all fields) so lack curiosity about the events that surround them that they are often taken by surprise.

And in that spirit, perhaps the Abbott government was the greatest possible manifestation of Horne's prescient vision.

———

It's a truism that Australian federal elections are never won, only lost; but never in Australia's history has a government been elected on so strong a platform of not being the previous one. What makes this epoch extraordinary, then, is the haste with which the marriage of the Abbott government and the Australian people soured. And the responsibility for that fell at the feet of one man.

While governments have always been at the beck and call of the powerful—after all, that's basically what 'powerful' means—it was almost refreshing to see a government willing to perform with such brazen disregard for the common good. More specifically, never before has a leader so clearly outlined his priorities by demonstrating how little the common good came into the equation.

---

1 Let's be honest, you knew exactly what this book was about the second you picked it up. Thanks for doing so, by the way. Very good of you, and don't think it's not appreciated.

This book tells the tale of a government that came into office to begin what was predicted to be the beginning of a conservative epoch, not least because the Opposition was so divided and scattered, and yet proceeded to collapse under the weight of the exact same internecine squabbling and political opportunism that destroyed its opponents. Furthermore, it will depict the way that the Abbott government used a combination of zealotry, single-mindedness and sheer gall to transform near-universal national goodwill into widespread condemnation. In fact, this might yet be the story of how Australian politics has come to be changed forever.

There's an upside, though: perhaps it took the predations of the Abbott government to teach Australia to give a shit about politics again.

———

Tony couldn't have done it alone, mind. He was aided and supported by his treasurer, the often-struggling Joe Hockey, and a front bench principally made up of ineffectual and superannuated MPs and senators chosen for loyalty rather than competence, and a back office with little interest in hearing dissenting opinion (or, for that matter, opinions at all), controlled by Abbott's chief of staff, the formidable Peta Credlin.

Looking into what at the time seemed a deeply optimistic crystal ball, I wrote a piece entitled 'Why an Abbott Victory Would Be Good'[2] for the website TheVine, published a few days before the federal election in September 2013. In that piece I made a few predictions regarding how things would

———

2   http://www.thevine.com.au/life/news/why-an-abbott-election-victory-would-be-good-20130905-264996/

shake out in the all-but-mathematically-certain event of the Coalition taking power:

> We already know [Abbott] can't open his mouth without saying the exact wrong thing. We already know that he's terrible on policy, can't think on his feet and dodges responsibility. At the moment he can largely get away with blaming the government; once he's Prime Minister, that's not an option anymore. He will look like what he is: a man of narrow views and narrower knowledge woefully out of his depth.
>
> And look at the Abbott front bench: it's a viper's nest. They're not supporting Abbott because they think he's an inspiring leader, since he's demonstrated comprehensively that he's not: they've backed him because the greatest strength they have had against Labor over the last 18 months has been in presenting a united front.
>
> Once they're in power this bunch of smart, ambitious and shrewd politicians are going to be a lot less forgiving of a leader who's an obvious and embarrassing liability. Hockey isn't going to fade back into the benches. Neither is [Malcolm] Turnbull. Neither is [Julie] Bishop. Neither is [Scott] Morrison. Those squabbles have been sublimated for the time being because they had a common enemy: Labor. Once in power, they'll have a different common enemy: each other.

At the time I wondered if I was simply whistling as I passed the graveyard of progressive Australian politics.

After all, the centre-left Labor Party was in complete disarray. In the event that the recently reinstated PM Kevin Rudd somehow managed to scrape home in that election, there was still no serious hope he would have a genuine majority and similarly little possibility that his government would do anything more than pander to the middle ground. Rudd was no negotiator, unlike his immediate predecessor and rival Julia

Gillard, and in any case the party was still riven by the leadership coup that had just reinstated him as leader.

Abbott, meanwhile, was declaring that the grown-ups
would be back in charge. By promising near-identical policies
to Labor on education, health, the National Broadband
Network and the National Disability Insurance Scheme,
and assuring electors they would keep a steady hand on the
economic tiller, the Liberal–National Coalition neatly delineated the choice between the parties: Labor offered crisis; the
Coalition offered unity.

However, barely had the new House of Representatives
formed than the government unmasked its neo-conservative
reformist agenda, one wildly different to the steady-as-she-
goes government promised during the campaign. In its battle
with Labor, the Coalition under Tony Abbott had pursued
victory with the same tenacity and zeal as a dog pursuing
a car—and, similarly, had seemingly not completely thought
through the consequences of victory.

———

Australia has suffered under unpopular leaders before, of
course. According to their detractors, Rudd was an arrogant
bully, Gillard a disloyal Judas, John Howard a fuddy-duddy,
Paul Keating a brawler, Bob Hawke a boozed-up union stooge,
Malcolm Fraser a manipulative snake and Gough Whitlam an
irresponsible idealist. However, one has to go all the way back
to Billy McMahon to find a prime minister who was so widely
considered by the electorate to be an actual fool. That is until . . .

The story upon which you're about to embark is one of a
government of blinkered visionaries, superannuated also-rans
and hard-nosed opportunists; of a gun-shy Opposition, unwilling

or unable to do more than run out the clock as the government scored own-goals; of a ragtag bunch of ideologues and neophytes in the Senate who somehow became the conscience of a nation, and for which they had to be punished. It is how political reality came to the major political parties and, for the most part, gave their legislative gonads a good, solid kicking.

It's the story of a government that turned Australia from a pioneer in renewable energy and climate change policy to an international laughing-stock, even being rightfully criticised by such high-volume polluters as China and the US. It's the story of how a government destroyed Australia's reputation as a nation of laconic, friendly she'll-be-right larrikins and transformed us into small-minded, human rights-averse xenophobes.

It's also the story of a government that was determined to apply to our enviable systems of socialised healthcare and education the same free-market policies as the United States, at exactly the same time as the US was socialising its health and education infrastructure in a desperate attempt to rectify the expensive, debt-heavy failures of their bloated, unsustainable, for-profit systems.

Not a bad effort for less than two years.

It's also a record of a period that I sincerely believe—or, at the very least, anxiously hope—will be looked back on as a tipping point for the workings of democracy in this wide, brown, sea-girt land.

For if there's one thing that the Abbott government did do, it was to teach the world something extraordinary about our lucky country: that we can never have things so good that we don't still inexplicably choose to fuck it all up.

1
THE GATHERING STORM

In which the auguries show stormy weather ahead for the
people of Australia

In order to explain how the Abbott government stumbled into power, it's important to give some context and outline how the nation had been faring during the previous few years. This is what the great playwrights call 'foreshadowing'.

In November 2007, the Labor government under Kevin Rudd had wiped out the Coalition government of John Howard. It seemed like the sort of thumping triumph that would not only usher in a new epoch for the party, following the end of Howard's eleven-year reign, but potentially consign the Liberal and National parties to history.

Hilarious though it may now seem, following the 2007 landslide there were high-minded editorials speculating on whether this marked the end of right-wing politics per se and heralded a new, less economically driven era in Australia, in which the debate would be less between the interests of employers versus the employed and more between maintaining jobs versus preserving the environment.

Oddly enough, this Labor-versus-Greens future has yet to pass, but many of the seeds of Labor's later problems were sown in its electoral triumph. First up, the party faced the problem of every party that wins a comprehensive victory after a long time in the wilderness: inevitably, the government benches were filled with a large, unwieldy collection of MPs. This wasn't unique; with any party in any epoch, this endless shifting of such an unbalanced load is part of what keeps the truck of Australian governance swerving wildly from left to right as it barrels down Democracy Highway.

Hence the Rudd benches were filled with new, inexperienced MPs who'd been plonked in the gig because of anger with the previous government rather than any particular local enthusiasm for the individual, mixed in with veteran incumbents terrified that this was their last chance to prove themselves and make their mark.

So far, so typical. What was unusual this time around was the new prime minister.

Kevin Rudd had already proved himself an ideas man during his relatively brief tenure in the federal party. He'd only entered the House of Representatives in 1998, after a stint in Queensland state politics serving as premier Wayne Goss's chief of staff. In 2001, he became Shadow Minister for Foreign Affairs and quickly gained a high profile, particularly after Australia entered the war in Iraq in 2003.[1]

---

1 What's not quite as often remembered is how Rudd made statements at the time such as: 'There is no debate or dispute as to whether Saddam Hussein possesses weapons of mass destruction. He does. There's no dispute as to whether he's in violation of UN Security Council resolutions. He is' (*Lateline*, ABC TV, 24 September 2002).

Rudd entered the shadow ministry when Simon Crean was leader; he continued under Mark Latham, despite having supported Latham's rival Kim Beazley when Crean resigned. When Latham led the party to defeat in 2004, Beazley was returned as leader unopposed, even though Rudd was now being touted as a possible contender. However, it seemed that Rudd was set to play a strong supporting role as a frontbencher in a future Beazley government. After all, given Labor's recent history, maybe it was time to get behind a consensus builder of the middle ground like Beazley rather than a Latham-style visionary hothead like Rudd, who already had a private reputation within the party for tantrum-throwing, not to mention a revolving door of staff.

However, by mid-2006 the polls were consistently showing higher public approval for the beaming, multilingual Queenslander than the stout, cautious Western Australian. As the year drew to a close, Beazley sought to end leadership speculation before preparations for the following year's election began in earnest. By calling for a leadership vote, Beazley placed his neck in a noose, and on 4 December, Labor had a new leader.

Rudd was beloved by a good slab of the public for his future-focused approach compared with the increasingly tired-looking Howard, who was widely (and, as it turned out, correctly) assumed to be planning to hand over the leadership to the even-less-beloved treasurer, Peter Costello, inside of twelve months in the event that he won the election. Even so, there were rumblings behind closed doors about Rudd's temper, his inability to delegate to others, and his refusal to brook dissent. However, he also looked like the man best suited to trounce the listing Coalition government. And on 24 November 2007, he did exactly that.

And that really should have been the end of the story of Rudd too: popular reformer makes popular reforms. And it's worth remembering that he actually did achieve much: there was the apology to the Stolen Generations, there was the ratification of the Kyoto Protocol after endless hedging by the Howard government, and there was even bipartisan support for an emissions trading scheme with the Coalition led by Malcolm Turnbull.

And there was something else that should have cemented Labor's hold on government in Australia for a generation: less than a year after Rudd took power, the world's economic system abruptly collapsed.

———

In 2008 something happened that should, had humans been rational creatures, have signalled the end of supply-side economics generally and the barely regulated global financial system specifically: a little hiccup that became the most destructive single economic event since the Great Depression of 1929. It was accurately called the Global Financial Crisis.

The causes were both insanely complicated (a credit crunch precipitated by unregulated overvaluation of sub-prime mortgages by bullish banks and investment firms) and exceedingly simple (unfettered greed), but the short version of the story is that banks, particularly in the US, had been playing an expensive game of musical chairs with the mortgage industry, and that when the music suddenly stopped they found themselves with no chairs, no cash and huge amounts of worthless debt they were never going to recover.

The effect went global as banks began to fall over, forcing governments to either bail them out or effectively renationalise them. Investment stopped dead, sending the poison way beyond the financial system and out into national economies. Few nations experienced any economic growth. China continued to expand positively, as did India and the petro-economies of the Middle East; but the US, UK, Russia, Iceland, New Zealand, Greenland, Canada, Mexico and just about all of the European Union countries were slammed. And yet through all this devastation, Australia just sorta toddled along.

Why? There are three main reasons, one vastly more important than the other two.

Least importantly, prices for commodities were good and high—especially iron ore, which Australia was exporting to the still-buying China. This was very convenient, absolutely, as the mining boom was providing Australia with a decent chunk of its export market. However, the benefits have been frequently overstated: sure, having China buy our stuff was very helpful to the national bottom line. But then again, the US, New Zealand, a good deal of Europe and—most significantly—Russia all had solid and undiminished commodities exports to China, and yet all still got hit hard by the GFC. Indeed, in the cases of South Africa, Ukraine and Canada, their major export was *specifically* iron ore, and they still took the crisis right in their collective geopolitical faces.

Another thing that cushioned the impact was that Australian banks were in a less-parlous state than those that had been free and easy with things like sub-prime mortgages. There had been complaints from the financial sector

through the eighties and nineties regarding the conservative regulatory approach employed by successive Australian
governments, which was criticised as financial timidity, but
those voices briefly went quiet once US banks started requiring expensive bailouts to stave off complete collapse.[2]

Thus what had previously seemed overcautious now proved
to have been prescient and prudent, and Australia's financial
system emerged as among the most robust in the world. So it
was down to good long-term management, eh? Well, yes, to
an extent . . . except that similar policies and reforms had been
instituted at around the same period as Australia in Canada,
Japan, Norway and New Zealand, and it didn't appear to help
them stave off recession when the GFC hit.

The third reason why Australia steered through the rocks of
crisis relatively unscathed was unique. While most other economies abruptly cut spending and instituted austerity measures
when the GFC hit, the Rudd government—and, the Treasury
under Wayne Swan—gave the economy a short, sharp shock.
In October 2008, the government announced a $10.3 billion
stimulus package to be given directly to Australian families,
followed by enormous and swift government investment in
infrastructure the following February.

This had a twofold effect. First, people had cash which
they promptly spent, which offset what would have otherwise
been a major slowdown in the high-employing retail sector.

Second, people who would have otherwise been unemployed
by industries that were slowing down found themselves working

---

2 Obviously, the financial sector absolutely learned its lesson and would never
contribute to an insane credit bubble again, as Sydney's housing market demonstrated as interest rates bottomed out in 2015 . . .

in government-supported areas such as construction. Also, it was a good, cheap time to do some infrastructure building because prices were low—a win-win for the nation. In this way Rudd and Swan acted decisively, allaying the problems before they had a chance to take effect. And it's worth noting, given the Coalition's later demonisation of the plan as being a dangerous waste of capital, that it was entirely supported at the time by the Nationals and the Liberals under Turnbull. (This was to become an issue for Turnbull later, however.)

Unfortunately, like disease immunisation programs, the stimulus package was the victim of its own success in that it avoided the terrifying dangers a little *too* well.

Like privileged parents deciding that measles can't really be that big a deal since they haven't met children blinded and brain-damaged by the disease, it was commonly assumed that the GFC was a damp squib since no-one saw banks collapsing and people losing their homes. Greeks are rioting in the streets? The US financial system is on the brink of collapse? Sure, but just look at how the government is spending *my* taxes!

Thus the narrative was not that the nation had been adeptly saved and that we suddenly had the strongest economy on the planet while the rest of the world was in turmoil; it was that the profligate spendthrift Labor government had pissed Australia's glorious surplus up against a wall in a showy popularity contest.

With the benefit of hindsight we can see the effect of the stimulus package more clearly, especially when we look at the effects of austerity on the rest of the world. In many cases, savage cuts to government spending helped create a furious underclass of people being punished further for already doing it tough, even while the people responsible for the GFC—the predatory investment companies and sub-prime lenders— took handsome bonuses from their employers following said employers' government bailouts. This realisation—that the rich and powerful were profiting from a system that was cutting basic services to citizens already finding it increasingly hard to make ends meet—did not land peacefully, as the emergence of the international Occupy movement demonstrated.

Iceland's government went broke. There were honest-to-god riots in the streets of London. New York's Wall Street was occupied for months at a time despite increasingly heavy-handed policing. Europe saw the popular return of the same odious nationalism that presaged the rise of fascism ahead of World War II, with openly racist political parties, such as Golden Dawn in Greece and UKIP in Britain, winning local elections.

Speaking of nationalism, Vladimir Putin handled the effects on Russia in classic USSR style: by distracting the populace with shiny new enemies—Gay people! Young people! Social justice charities! All-girl punk bands!—and introducing heavy-handed new legislation against them before launching a military takeover of the Crimean peninsula from the economically ravaged Ukraine.

More recently, Greece's position as part of the European Union still remains shaky, following its new government's demand to restructure its debt arrangements. The class tensions in the United States, exacerbated by the widening gulf between rich and poor, have seen an unprecedented rise in police shootings of poor (i.e. black) men, and the rise of the #blacklivesmatter movement.

Almost a decade on from the GFC, it's still having a tangible influence on the politics, the economics and the day-to-day lives of a significant portion of the world.

In Australia, it barely registered at all.

————

By 2010, the government should have been crowing about having saved the nation from certain economic destruction. However, things proceeded to go exceptionally wrong for the prime ministership of Kevin Rudd.

The spirit of bipartisanship that had seen the government and Opposition unite to save Australia from the GFC, and which seemed poised to provide decisive positive action on climate change, had collapsed after a Liberal Party leadership challenge in November 2009 in which Turnbull and his main challenger, Joe Hockey, were both blindsided by a surprise challenger named Tony Abbott.

You may have heard of him.

Hockey was eliminated from the running early, and then Abbott took the leadership from Turnbull by a single vote— and promptly interpreted this slim victory as an unquestionable mandate for his singular vision.[3]

Abbott had no intention of supporting any sort of carbon price or emissions trading scheme, having memorably declared climate change science to be both 'highly contentious' and, in less thoughtful terms, as 'absolute crap' earlier that year. He pushed Rudd to declare an early election and take the issue

———————————————

3   Remember that thing earlier about foreshadowing?

to the people, and then painted Rudd's refusal to acquiesce as cowardice. He could do this because Rudd's position within the Labor Party was becoming untenable.

Previously private complaints were starting to leak to the public indicating that the Prime Minister's Office was micromanaging portfolios, ignoring backbenchers and making policy decisions without warning, much less consulting the ministers responsible for implementing them. What was especially frustrating was that in doing so Rudd was ignoring his actual responsibilities, leaving important things undone.

His brusqueness and temper rubbed party and parliamentary colleagues the wrong way, leaving his long-suffering deputy, Julia Gillard, to put out fires, smooth ruffled feathers and mix multiple metaphors.

When word circulated that Rudd's chief of staff was canvassing the levels of party support for the PM, Gillard decided enough was enough. On 23 June she called for a leadership ballot and, with the numbers clearly against him, Rudd stepped down rather than face a poll.

The popular and capable Gillard was elected to the leadership unopposed and was sworn in as the nation's twenty-seventh prime minister the following day. She graciously granted Rudd the Foreign Affairs portfolio, and there was genuine hope that maybe things would settle down.

Those hopes proved to be . . . let's go with 'optimistic'.

———

Before we delve too far into Labor's race to self-destruction, let's focus on one of the oddest spinoffs of the GFC: it made economic rock stars out of mining barons.

This was especially true of billionaire resource magnates Gina Rinehart and Clive Palmer, who were wealthy and therefore both virtuous and wise, and who were thus taken inexplicably seriously as economic and political pundits.

Rinehart's political activities were limited mainly to donating heavily to the Coalition and occasionally penning screeds for the more conservative press, railing against the lazy classes who didn't have the gumption to follow her example and pull themselves up by their bootstraps and put their shoulder to the grindstone. Somehow she failed to mention the arguably decisive ingredient in her own success, which was: 'inherit an enormous mining empire from one's father'.

That's not to diminish her literary efforts, though. Rinehart's restless muse was responsible for 'Our Future', which—like all great poetry—was unveiled to the world via a plaque riveted to a thirty-tonne iron ore boulder plonked outside of a shopping centre. In the event that you're not conveniently reading this while visiting Coventry Square Markets in Morley, Western Australia, be advised that the poem rails against 'political hacks' who are 'unleashing rampant tax'.

Clive Palmer, however, had bigger dreams than merely reshaping our nation's geographical and literary landscape. He'd been a member of the National Party in Queensland for two decades (and of the Liberal National Party following the 2008 merger of both parties) and been one of its largest financial backers, but he then clashed with premier Campbell Newman, who became premier in 2012, over planned increases in coal royalties (which would cost the mining baron dearly) and his brutal and unpopular state budget.

After much public criticism of the LNP generally and Newman in particular, Palmer was asked to resign from the party in September, which he publicly refused to do—adorably declaring that 'threats are part of a democracy' and beginning a legal challenge with the party over whether or not they could suspend his life membership.

However, in what was to become an excitingly regular move over the subsequent years, he then performed an abrupt about face in November, quitting on the eve of a vote to expel him from the party. In his LNP-slamming statement upon his departure, Palmer declared that the problem with politics was that the wealthy and influential had too much sway, telling the ABC: 'Where you can pay money to put your cause regardless of the lobbyist's belief, I think that's a bad thing.'[4]

He also ruled out any plans to enter politics himself as an independent—a promise that turned out to be a tad disingenuous, since that very month rumours filtered through that he sought to resurrect the United Australia Party, the old-school conservative political warhorse that was dissolved after a mere fourteen years in 1945, when its remnants were absorbed into Menzies' new Liberal Party.

It was assumed at first that Palmer's new political party would see him join fellow ex-National Party member and Queensland maverick Bob Katter.[5] However, by April 2013 it was revealed that he was the proud owner of the shiny new

---

4   Yeah, he actually said that in an interview that also contained the declaration: 'The government of Queensland, I believe, is too heavily influenced by lobbyists and by business' (ABC TV, 22 November 2012). Monocle-wearers, apologies for your eyewear having no doubt just landed in your soup.
5   'Maverick' might be an understatement. After all, this is a man who threw eggs at the Beatles during their 1964 Brisbane visit.

Palmer United Party, which was set to field Senate candidates in every state in the upcoming election.[6]

Among those candidates were a former Queensland rugby league star, an ex-servicewoman with a history of disputes with the Department of Veterans Affairs and a Palmer-employed resources company CEO. This diverse group of political neophytes were to become rather better known a few months later.

———

After barely scraping through the election she called in 2010 shortly after assuming power, Gillard endured more vitriol and open aggression from within and without the government than any prime minister in Australian history, so it's important to remember a few things.

First, she successfully managed a minority government in the lower house and a Senate controlled by the crossbench through deft and regular negotiation which continued even after Labor had a workable majority in their own right following the elevation of Liberal defector Peter Slipper to the Speaker of the House. This was helped by the fact that her priority through this period was building consensus rather than embarking on ideologically driven crusades.

The second thing to note is that the Gillard government passed a staggering 543 pieces of legislation, an average of an

---

6 Apparently the reason he went with Palmer United was to distinguish the PUP from the Uniting Australia Party, who are notable entirely for having a name similar to the United Australia Party. However, it hasn't prevented Palmer trading on the (original) UAP's reputation, claiming that former PMs Joseph Lyons, Robert Menzies and Billy Hughes had been former Palmer party leaders. You can pull the same trick by calling your next group the Beatles and insisting your former bandmates include John Lennon and George Harrison. Watch out for Bob Katter, mind.

Act every two days in office, the highest rate of any Australian government in history.

Unfortunately the public perception was not that Gillard was a master negotiator and a skilled administrator of the nation, but that she was an uncomfortable-looking, childless, unmarried, atheist harridan with a weird drawly accent who lied about introducing a carbon tax. Attempts to make her more appealing to Middle Australia only made the problem worse, especially when she spoke out against gay marriage being legislated in Australia: a subject about which she'd been outspokenly and consistently in favour since her university days. It seemed like a transparent attempt to convince the electorate that she wasn't a terrifying leftie, largely because it was, but all it did was disappoint her supporters while failing to win over her detractors.

There was also the destabilising campaign being run against her within the party as Rudd engineered his return to the top spot, challenging and winning the leadership back in 2013.[7] It was a Pyrrhic victory, since by this stage it was already clear that Labor was doomed whether Gillard or Rudd were at the helm. Barring some extraordinary fluke of distributions, or perhaps a well-timed meteor strike, Tony Abbott would be Australia's next PM.

The meteor never came.

———

It's also important to remember how effective Tony Abbott was as Leader of the Opposition—a position, crucially, that doesn't

---

7   This entire episode is elegantly and passionately explored in Kerry-Anne Walsh's 2013 book, *The Stalking of Julia Gillard*. There's a solid chance that you've already read it if you're reading this: hell, it's a bestseller. Seriously, how good is it? Let's read it again and start a book club. We can do this book next.

require one to lead so much as attack. Attacking was where both Abbott and Morrison shone. Both had risen to their positions not through exemplary leadership or strength of vision but through their resolute ability to bring down those who dared stand between them and what they figured was rightfully theirs.

Abbott also successfully neutralised those opposed to him by ensuring that the Coalition went to the polls with essentially the same policies as Labor, thereby making it a choice between a government in disarray and a party promising unity, strength and quiet dignity.

That was easily accepted because few people had noticed Abbott's endorsement of the seventy-five-point plan presented by the Institute of Public Affairs, the staunchly neo-conservative think tank that had been instrumental in creating the modern Liberal Party in 1945 after the implosion of the United Australia Party, and had acted as the unofficial policy (and, historically, fundraising) arm of the Liberals ever since.

Its plan was outlined in an August 2012 article, provocatively titled 'Be Like Gough: 75 radical ideas to transform Australia', written by the IPA's executive director John Roskam, deputy executive director James Paterson and policy director Chris Berg, and published in the IPA's magazine.[8] In case you're not in the mood to check the list out, it's a series of very familiar-looking policies. Many were subsequently passed:

1. Repeal the carbon tax, and don't replace it
2. Abolish the Department of Climate Change

---

8 At the time this wish list read like a neocon wet dream. These days it looks like what it was: a list of specific instructions for the forthcoming Abbott government to enact.

30. Cease subsidising the car industry
43. Repeal the mining tax
44. Devolve environmental approvals for major projects to the states
47. Cease funding the Australia Network
49. Privatise Medibank.

Some were partially achieved:

3. Abolish the Clean Energy Fund
18. Eliminate family tax benefits
23. End mandatory disclosures on political donations
50. Break up the ABC and put out to tender each individual function
52. Reduce the size of the public service from current levels of more than 260,000 to at least the 2001 low of 212,784
53. Repeal the Fair Work Act
60. Remove all remaining tariff and non-tariff barriers to international trade
64. End all hidden protectionist measures, such as preferences for local manufacturers in government tendering
69. Immediately halt construction of the National Broadband Network and privatise any sections that have already been built.

Others were attempted but failed:

4. Repeal Section 18C of the Racial Discrimination Act
5. Abandon Australia's bid for a seat on the United Nations Security Council
6. Repeal the renewable energy target
11. Introduce fee competition to Australian universities
12. Repeal the National Curriculum
29. Eliminate the National Preventative Health Agency
72. Privatise the CSIRO.

None of these, except for the carbon and mining tax repeals, were taken to the election, not least because the party correctly realised that there would be little public support for such policies. However, as the above demonstrates, these were clearly things with which the Liberals enthusiastically agreed.

Furthermore, in April 2013, Tony Abbott had assured the IPA that he would take their instructions on board. In a speech celebrating the seventieth anniversary of the organisation, the soon-to-be PM closed his speech with the following shout-out to Roskam:

> You had a great deal of advice for me in that particular issue [of the *IPA Review*] and I want to assure you that the Coalition will indeed repeal the carbon tax, abolish the Department of Climate Change, abolish the Clean Energy Fund. We will repeal Section 18C of the Racial Discrimination Act, at least in its current form. We will abolish new health and environmental bureaucracies. We will deliver one billion dollars in red-tape savings every year. We will develop northern Australia. We will repeal the mining tax. We will create a one-stop shop for environmental approvals. We will privatise Medibank Private. We will trim the public service and we will stop throwing good money after bad on the NBN. So, ladies and gentlemen, that is a big 'yes' to many of the seventy-five specific policies you urged upon me in that particular issue of the magazine—but Gough Whitlam I will never be![9]

One thing noted at the time of the 2013 elections as an interesting quirk rather than a harbinger of doom was that dissatisfaction with Kevin Rudd did not seem to translate into support for Tony Abbott.

---

9 There's a video of this entire speech on the IPA's website, and it's important to be aware of it since it puts the lie to the government's subsequent insistence that these changes were because of Labor's profligate spendthriftery and not because they were clearly delineated policy decisions made long before the election was called.

Even a week out from the election, with the Coalition on a two-party preferred vote of 54 per cent to Labor's 46, the leaders were even closer in terms of voter dissatisfaction: Rudd on 58 per cent and Abbott on 51. Only 41 per cent of the electorate—an electorate that was clearly just about to vote the Coalition into power—claimed to be satisfied with Abbott's leadership, which still put him above Rudd's anaemic 32.

Even supporters of the Liberal Party were less than enthusiastic about its leader. On 4 May an opinion piece by *The Australian*'s Peter van Onselen was published under the headline: ABBOTT LOOKS SET TO BECOME A DO-NOTHING PM. It castigated the leader for his failure to adhere to a consistent position—'the policy goals Abbott has announced so far cut unsatisfactorily across conservative and liberal principles'—and correctly pointed out that he couldn't possibly promise lower taxes and at the same time support such things as a Medicare levy to fund the National Disability Insurance Scheme.

What van Onselen didn't realise—along with the rest of the nation—was that these things weren't in fact contradictions, or weaknesses, or misunderstandings. There was a far more straightforward explanation: they were lies.

Few questions were asked before the election as to how exactly the Abbott government hoped to the fulfil its pledge to be a steady, no-surprises government with no cuts to services, reductions in personal tax and increased spending in the various large-scale programs which they supposedly supported along with Labor, such as the Gonksi education reforms that called for a massive redistribution of education funding, the National Disability Insurance Scheme, the National Broadband Network and others.

It turned out that the plan was to not worry about any of them.

———

So the question could be asked: given that this was the plan, and that the Coalition had victory assured, why on earth did Abbott not think to mention this stuff before the election?

Obviously, part of it was to neutralise Labor's remaining policy advantages, since Australia still thought it was getting an NBN, the NDIS and, as Abbott memorably declared, 'No cuts to health, no cuts to education, no change to pensions, no change to the GST and no cuts to the ABC or SBS.'[10]

But given the mess that Labor was in—a party in disarray, desperately clinging to a demonstrably dysfunctional leader with a divided backbench and a confused and terrified ministry—the Coalition could have waltzed into power while waving the IPA document as a policy statement, secure in the knowledge that Labor provided no serious alternative for most of the electorate.

Furthermore, this would have provided a handy piece of evidence to support the subsequent cries of 'Mandate!' upon which the government was to increasingly rely as the Senate and public rejected the legislative changes that had been assiduously hidden from them in the lead up to the polls.

Still, as the old saying goes, it's better to beg forgiveness than ask permission. And as the new government was about to demonstrate, it had no intention of doing either.

---

10 He stated this to SBS *News* in September 2013. Seriously, check it out on YouTube: it's the most bare-faced piece of professional fibsmanship you're ever likely to see. Incidentally, by the time Joe Hockey flagged his desire to raise the GST in April 2015, every single one of those promises would be comprehensively broken. Which, technically, is kind of an impressive achievement. Technically.

2
MEET THE MOTLEY CREW

In which the captain commissions his shipmates

Nothing unites a party quite like victory, and it was a united and emboldened Coalition that formed the first Abbott ministry.

There were few surprises among the frontbenchers; many of the positions had been flagged far earlier, with most—but not all—of the shadow ministers reprising their portfolios but in bigger, nicer offices.

The nineteen-strong ministry was immediately controversial, principally for containing exactly one person without a penis: the deputy leader and foreign minister, Western Australian MP Julie Bishop.

It was demonstrative of the Coalition's change in attitude now that they were in power since Bishop had been one of five women in the shadow ministry. Three of those shadow ministers were subsequently given junior portfolios to keep them out of the way while the big boys did the important work:

Sussan Ley as Assistant Minister for Education, Marise Payne in Human Services and Fiona Nash as Assistant Minister for Health.

But back to the front bench.

Bishop had enjoyed a chequered career, first with an undistinguished stint as Minister for Ageing under John Howard from 2003 to 2006, followed by a rocky year as Minister for Education until the government's 2007 removal. Her time as shadow treasurer was similarly poor, including the embarrassing revelation that her chapter in 2008's *Liberals and Power: The road ahead* had been a) lifted almost word-for-word from a 1999 speech by businessman Roger Kerr, and b) allegedly written by her chief of staff Murray Hansen rather than Bishop herself. However, she'd seemingly found her metier as shadow foreign minister.

Nationals' leader Warren Truss was, as per convention, made deputy prime minister, or head of the kids' table at the Coalition's Christmas dinner. He was given the Infrastructure and Regional Development portfolio on top of his other duties, such as providing inspirational leadership for his own party—most notably demonstrated in the ABC's 2015 documentary series *The Nationals* when it was revealed that he had to be convinced by the party machine to take on leadership of the Nationals in 2007 after Mark Vaile retired and no-one else wanted the gig.

New South Wales hardliner Scott Morrison walked straight into the Immigration portfolio, having kept the government's hysteria about the threat of asylum seekers swarming Australia in boats at a fever pitch throughout the election campaign. An outspoken Christian, he broke from the popular Catholicism of the front bench to follow a charismatic Pentecostal faith at his Shirelive Church in Sutherland—a faith which apparently saw no contradiction between the words of Jesus Christ and performing dangerous and (at the time) illegal turnbacks of refugee vessels at sea, and that sort of personal comfort with hypocrisy was to become even more useful as time went on. He'd maintained a virulently anti-refugee line in Opposition, and was now in a position to turn rhetoric to policy. You know, because Jesus surely didn't expect one to love *all* those neighbours as thyself, did He?

New South Wales' Joe Hockey was appointed treasurer in what was either an olive branch or a poisoned chalice to a man who honestly, inexplicably thought he was destined to be the nation's leader one day. According to Madonna King's often-hilarious 2014 biography, *Not Your Average Joe*, when he challenged Malcolm Turnbull for the leadership, Abbott had pledged to support him against the leader and then unexpectedly run himself—reportedly after the Right faction of the party got cold feet about Hockey and Turnbull supporting the seditious notion of renewable energy. Hockey learned his lesson, though: by May 2013 he was telling the ABC, 'I find those wind turbines around Lake George to be utterly offensive,' and flagging his plans to scrap the Clean Energy Regulator.

———

One of the other elevations to the front bench raised eyebrows as Abbott made use of the old adage about keeping one's friends close and enemies closer.

The presence of Malcolm Turnbull in the Communications portfolio seemed like a manifestation of the latter. Turnbull had been shadow treasurer under leader Brendan Nelson—the man he successfully challenged for leadership—but after Abbott knocked him from the perch he was given the shadow portfolio of Communications. It was a perfect place to put someone whose ambitions seemed a little too close to the surface: a portfolio where, like Health or Human Services, it was easy to publicly screw up, but difficult to shine—especially since the portfolio had traditionally been under the thumb of the Prime Minister's Office.

Some of the other appointments were little more than a thank you to long-serving allies. Several Howard-era over-stayers were moved into what amounted to honorary roles—most notably Bronwyn Bishop, who was given the Speaker's chair in the House of Representatives,[1] while Philip Ruddock was appointed Chief Whip.

The appointment of Victorian Howard-era never-quite-was Kevin Andrews to the Social Services portfolio was an early indication of the seriousness with which Abbott took the treatment of the nation's unemployed and pensioners: putting them in the hands of the man who'd so comprehensively fumbled the ball on the workplace reform-a-palooza that was WorkChoices.

A similar anti-superstar was selected for the Health and Sport portfolios—Queensland ghost Peter Dutton. He also chose to abstain from the apology to the Stolen Generations—a move that remained his most notable activity in parliament until being made assistant treasurer in the Howard ministry,

---

1   At the risk of jumping ahead, it turned out that this didn't work out all that well. There's a whole chapter on it coming up.

and then kinda hanging around until being given the front bench gig. Little did anyone know that his first year in the role would see him declared the Worst Health Minister in Living Memory by the readers of industry journal *Australian Doctor*.

Fellow Queenslander George Brandis became the nation's attorney-general and, inexplicably, Minister for the Arts, but where Dutton was relatively quiet about which groups of people he didn't much care for, Brandis was perfectly happy to, for example, insist that the Greens were actually Nazis and that the childless and unmarried Julia Gillard had no place talking about whether it was inappropriate to tell children not to have premarital sex—as Abbott had done—since she'd never even been married, the *slattern*.

Victorian MP Greg Hunt had studied at Melbourne Law School and was a Fulbright scholar at Yale, and had co-written a prize-winning thesis entitled A Tax to Make the Polluter Pay about the spectacularly prescient idea of putting a 'tax' on emissions—such as, let's just say, of 'carbon'. However, he'd since learned to keep his love of science to his damn self, which was good since he was given the job of environment minister, a portfolio that always seemed to have invisible quote marks around it. He would have the job of enacting the ludicrous Direct Action policy, a strategy that he was clearly smart enough to know couldn't possibly work and which he therefore defended largely by blinking.

South Australia's Christopher Pyne was given the Education and Training portfolio. He was one of the youngest MPs in Australian political history when elected in 1993, at the tender age of twenty-five, and therefore had a great sense of what it was like to go straight from private school to university to Parliament without any of that annoying 'actual life experience' nonsense in between. He'd been a moderate in his younger days, but a stint on the backbenches during the Howard years taught him that no-one likes actual liberals in the Liberal Party. Pyne also held a grudge against Julie Bishop, having unsuccessfully challenged for the deputy leadership under Brendan Nelson (where he won the smallest vote of the three candidates, reflecting the high esteem in which his colleagues held him).

New Minister for Employment Eric Abetz didn't let the fact that his family had flourished thanks to finding a new life in Australia after World War II stop him from siding with the government's harsh treatment of asylum seekers and refugees, possibly because his great-uncle Otto Abetz isn't a household name—at least, not outside those households that like to keep track of former SS officers sentenced for war crimes. That also didn't stop him branding the Greens as dangerous extremists during his Howard-era gig as forestry minister, although his finest moment was to come. At this point, no-one expected the employment minister to openly support the comprehensively debunked 'link' between abortion and breast cancer on national television as an expression of his anti-choice views ahead of the World Conference of Families conservative Christian conference in August 2014. You may justifiably wonder why exactly the employment minister was weighing in on the subject at all, of course.

———

There were a few absences from the Abbott front bench though: one predictable, two perhaps less so.

South Australian senator Cory Bernardi had been Abbott's parliamentary secretary and a close and trusted friend and colleague. He would have reasonably expected a ministerial berth had he not unwisely made the objectively ludicrous declaration that the increasing calls for same-sex marriage in Australia were obviously the precursor to calls to legalise polygamy and bestiality.

'The next step, quite frankly, is having three people or four people that love each other being able to enter into a permanent union endorsed by society or any other type of relationship,' he breathlessly declared during a senatorial debate in September 2012. 'There are even some creepy people out there . . . [who] say it is okay to have consensual sexual relations between humans and animals . . . I think that these things are the next step.' (Of course, such a next step would require animals to also be deemed adults and to be either legal citizens or to be issued government visas in order to be eligible to wed under Australian law, so Bernardi probably doesn't have to worry about his horrific vision of terrifying animal unions until dogs successfully agitate for the right to vote.)

Despite doubling down on the comments on ABC radio on 19 September ('We've already had complaints from those in the polyamorous community about [how] this will discriminate against them,' he implausibly insisted, 'and I don't know where it will end'), Bernardi resigned from his position later that afternoon and headed to the backbenches, where he would remain when the party took government, despite his closeness to the PM.

Also missing from the ministry was Victorian MP Sophie Mirabella, who had held the shadow portfolio of Innovation, Industry, Science and Research and would probably have walked into the Industry portfolio—thereby immediately doubling the number of women on the front bench. However, through a combination of declining support for the Liberals in the seat, her personal unpopularity and some less-than-brilliant public moments (notably, like Dutton, she was absent at the 2008 apology to the Stolen Generations), she lost her historically safe Liberal seat of Indi to independent candidate Cathy McGowan. Embarrassingly for the ambitious Mirabella, this gave her the distinction of being the sole sitting Liberal MP to lose her seat in the 2013 election. That takes some doing.

There was another absence from the front bench that surprised no-one more than the man himself: outspoken Queensland senator Ian Macdonald. We will come to this again in a little bit.

One of the instructions the IPA had issued in its 'Be Like Gough' article was number 59: 'Halve the size of the Coalition front bench from 32 to 16.' They didn't quite get there—the Abbott front bench was initially nineteen—but they did feel a great need to drag a few ministries that had existed under their predecessors out to the kerb.

Climate Change was a predictable casualty, but Aged Care was perhaps a more surprising one given the concerns about Australia's steadily greying population. Water was also off the list, subsumed into the Environment portfolio.

However, the most telling elimination was that of the Science portfolio, which was no longer to be a stand-alone ministry but was rolled over into that of Industry, which was to be the purview of a Queensland Liberal National Party MP, the economically hard-right Ian Macfarlane.

———

And then there was the prime minister's chief of staff, Peta Credlin. Abbott's nickname for her is the 'force majeure'. It's a term that literally means both 'superior force' and, in contract law and insurance parlance, 'unavoidable accident'.

Credlin was a more experienced politician than a good deal of the parliamentary party when the Abbott-led Coalition won government. She'd been a staffer for Senator Kay Patterson in 1999 before getting a plum job as adviser to communications minister Richard Alston in the Howard government and then leaving to work for Racing Victoria. Along the way she wed the Liberal Party's federal director, Brian Loughnane (the story goes that she was set up by Kay Patterson with the instructions 'you need to marry this man'), and when she got sick of commuting between her job in Melbourne and Canberra, where her husband was, she took up adviser gigs working for two Liberal senators, Robert Hill and Helen Coonan.

When Rudd swept to power, she briefly went back into the racing arena, but was coaxed back to be a staffer for the new leader, Brendan Nelson. It's a testament to her tenacity and ability that she became chief of staff to the party's next leader, Malcolm Turnbull, when he beat Nelson. When Abbott subsequently beat Turnbull, she slotted straight into the chief of staff position for Abbott. Indeed, it's hard to avoid the conclusion that Credlin has been leading the Liberal Party for longer than the last three actual leaders.

As something of an indication of what fate befalls those who cross her, it's noteworthy that her relationship with Turnbull turned frosty soon after he became leader but, significantly, she was demoted and not sacked, possibly because to dismiss her would have destroyed the never-convivial relationship between Turnbull and Loughnane. But no sooner had the rest of Turnbull's former team had their farewell drinks than news came through that Abbott had chosen her as his new chief of staff.

At the risk of jumping ahead, the PM was to prove remarkably loyal to his chief of staff, even standing up to demands she be let go by no less an authority than Rupert Murdoch (who imparted his commands via Twitter, lest there be any confusion over his intent). That said, one has to wonder if he was motivated less by loyalty and more by fear of what would happen without her in his corner. Indeed, in 2011 Brandis told Australian journalist Kate Legge approvingly that 'Tony routinely refers to her as "the boss",' for Legge's eye-opening *Weekend Australian* profile on Credlin that November, while Greg Hunt said of Abbott, 'I think he's slightly afraid of her.' And he was right to be, according to Seven Network's Mark Riley, since she wasn't above giving the leader a swift and very literal kick if she felt he was speaking out of turn.[2] And Abbott's clearly not the only one: Legge wryly noted that outspoken and dedicated Abbott supporters Greg Hunt, Brendan Nelson,

---

2 'We were having a couple of beers and a chat about the trip to Afghanistan, and [Abbott] made a couple of remarks that she thought were just a little bit out of school. She gave him a swift kick in the shin. It was done with good humour, but for us, it was a really interesting insight into their relationship' (Riley, 'Ms Fix-it', *Sydney Morning Herald*, 4 April 2014).

George Brandis, Scott Morrison and Andrew Robb all just so happened to ring to emphasise just how nifty Credlin is.

Margie Abbott and then-New South Wales Premier Barry O'Farrell both confessed to being scared of her (again, no doubt for being so nice!), while an anonymous Liberal, who clearly knew better than to go on record, asked Legge: 'Who is going to shirtfront Loughnane with complaints about his wife and vice versa?'[3]

And that was the way things were balancing in September 2013, when the party realised that they had a leader kept on a short leash by his chief of staff, about which the only possible recourse was to appeal to the party's director: her husband.

'There is an unwritten rule that the party keeps an eye on the prime minister's office, and the prime minister's office keeps an eye on the party,' another wisely anonymous former party official told Fairfax's Jane Cadzow in April 2014. 'It makes it pretty much impossible for that to happen when you have this watertight connection between the federal director and the prime minister's chief of staff.'

Even when the party was in Opposition there were complaints about Credlin's management style, indicated by the steady flow of resignations from the office. Backbenchers were frustrated at the lack of access to the leader and the sharp texts they received from his chief of staff about perceived failures and disloyalty.

———

Once the Coalition took power, Credlin didn't waste any time in exercising her authority. Her first major move was to

---

3 'Shirtfront' was evidently a popular verb in Abbott circles.

veto ministerial staffing choices as the new ministers started setting up their offices (and, in Brandis's case, acquiring exorbitantly expensive bookcases).[4]

Abetz was made to demote his long-time chief of staff Chris Fryar when he was given the Employment portfolio, on the orders of the PM's Office. Similarly, Treasurer Joe Hockey's choice of foreign investment adviser, former Victorian MP Victor Perton, was knocked back, as was Assistant Treasurer Arthur Sinodinos's choice of chief of staff.

When Sussan Ley took the Health portfolio in December 2014, she was immediately informed that her long-time chief of staff Rowena Cowen was not going to be joining her, while other ministers (including finance minister Mathias Cormann, Nationals MP and agriculture minister Barnaby Joyce and her old boss, communications minister Malcolm Turnbull) also discovered they had new, Credlin-approved staff in their offices.

She also made sure that those who had displeased her knew what was what. For example, the aforementioned Senator Ian Macdonald, the venerable LNP senator who had assumed he'd be waltzing into the Regional Development portfolio until he suffered one of the 'worst days of his life' and was told that his services would not be required on the front bench.[5]

---

4   Got some books that need shelving? The attorney-general probably has some room on the $15,000 custom-built set of bookshelves you helped pay for. At that price, we assume that it conceals a secret door that swings open to allow George access to the Brandiscave.

5   'What should have been one of the proudest days of my life has turned into one of the worst. The ecstasy of a new government and success in the north has turned a little sad with a phone call from Tony Abbott saying he has no room for me in the new ministry' ('Worst day of my life', *Sydney Morning Herald*, 15 September 2013).

Within months Macdonald was publicly attributing the snub to interference from the PM's office.[6] He became outspoken about the 'almost obsessive centralised control phobia over . . . every aspect of Parliament' and declared that 'I was not elected to this Parliament by the Prime Minister's Office, but by the Liberal National Party of Queensland and by the voters of Queensland'.

There's another slightly less conspiratorial interpretation, of course: perhaps, like his pal Cory Bernardi, he'd made a noose for his own neck with some colourfully inaccurate public statements, like his declaration that the political activism group GetUp! was 'the Hitler Youth wing of the Greens political movement'.[7] Stuff like that did him few favours and made him look like some sort of loose cannon, prone to saying ridiculous things in Parliament.

But for the time being, Bernardi, Macdonald and everyone else were prepared to preserve party unity. For the time being.

---

6   He didn't mince words either, snarling, 'I'll not have unelected advisers in the Prime Minister's Office telling elected politicians, who are actually in touch with their constituencies, what should or shouldn't be done' (ABC *News*, 4 December 2013).

7   Yeah, he did really say that ('Greens and GetUp! demand apology', *Herald Sun*, 3 November 2011). What other adorably barking things will Senator Macdonald inexplicably say to other adults in Parliament? Keep reading to find out! Maybe there'll be some sort of prize for catching them all, like crazy, offensive Pokemon.

3
MANDATE, MANDATE, MANDATE!

In which the captain sets sail with the wind at his back

It was an excited and energised new government that leaped into action in September 2013, dismissing all criticisms over pointless things like 'only having one woman on the front bench' (even when that criticism came from his own Senator Sue Boyce,[1] who described herself as 'shocked and embarrassed by the Liberal Party' over the apparent gender-based snub).[2] This was a government that knew it had no time to

---

1   And here's as good as place as any to repeat Abbott's undergraduate statement that 'it would be folly to expect that women would ever approach equal representation in a large number of areas simply because their aptitudes, their abilities and interests are different for physiological reasons'. And sure, we all say stupid things when we're at uni, but we would probably think it shrewd to disown them when specifically asked about them on *Four Corners*—which the PM did not in March 2010.

2   WA Liberal MP Denis Jensen also claimed that the ministries were not being decided on merit. That said, he may have been smarting from not having been appointed science minister (a role he had his eye on), possibly because that position no longer existed.

waste in enacting the agenda that it had . . . well, not taken to the electorate, per se, but at least had discussed with the IPA beforehand.

One thing that Abbott didn't do in his first week in the job was head up north to spend quality time with the Yolngu people of north-eastern Arnhem Land. Which was odd, since mere weeks before the election the then-Opposition leader had attended the Garma Festival and clumsily asked community leader Galarrwuy Yunupingu: 'And why not, if you will permit me; why shouldn't I, if you will permit me; spend my first week as prime minister, should that happen, on this, on your country.' To which Yunupingu, imagining the offer was genuine, had agreed.

While the Senate was still being sorted out—a subject to which we shall return (and oh, there's a *lot* to talk about . . .)—it was clear even on election night that the government wouldn't have an upper house majority. This was in no way to diminish the cries of 'Mandate!' that were to ring throughout Canberra in the subsequent months, such as in the new PM's poetic declaration that, 'In the end I think they all need to respect the government of our nation has a mandate and the parliament should work with the government of the day to implement its mandate.'

Abbott had made clear that he wasn't simply going to pander to the Coalition's base in his first term of rule. 'A good government is one that governs for all Australians, including those that haven't voted for it,' he declared in his victory speech, which was interpreted at the time as meaning that he'd be governing for all when in fact he was implying that the new government wasn't intending to worry too much about being good.

That description of 'good government' would be an interesting one, since it turned out that was apparently not to start until 9 February 2015. But let's not get ahead of ourselves!

———

First up, as with any big move, there was some housecleaning to do.

The government made clear that it wasn't about to waste any time exacting revenge on those it felt had earned it. Former Victorian Labor premier Steve Bracks was informed by foreign minister Julie Bishop that his services were no longer required as Australia's consul-general in New York, because his appointment had clearly been political—unlike, obviously, his dismissal.

New immigration minister Scott Morrison was also hitting the ground running, announcing that he would be reviewing a new efficient processing system for asylum seekers based on the 'Detained Fast Track' system the UK had adopted, a system praised by Human Rights Watch as being 'inherently unsuitable for complex cases' and 'not rigorous enough to meet basic standards of fairness', and for being particularly poor with regard to assessment of cases involving 'trafficking for sexual or labor exploitation, forced marriage, forced sterilization, domestic violence, female genital mutilation, threat of "honor" killings and rape'. (This system would later appear to be fair and humane compared with the laws that Morrison was to later introduce—but we don't want to give away the surprise!)

The board of the National Broadband Network also warned communications minister Malcolm Turnbull, who had criticised them at length in the press, that they would resign rather than see the program be officially demolished—at least, the Labor-supported version of it that used current technology rather than the existing 'copper network' (which had replaced the previous 'cans and string' network).

Attorney-General George Brandis also started one of his long games with the announcement that he would launch an inquiry into how to reform the Senate—purely in the interests of representative democracy, to be clear, and not because the government wanted to minimise the possibility of crossbenchers mucking up their aforementioned mandate. He also began exploring the possibility of making it illegal for groups and individuals to begin public boycotts on environmental grounds, painting the environmental movement as a bunch of selfish bullies unfairly tormenting the planet's plucky corporations.

Education minister Christopher Pyne got straight into attacking universities for forcing students to pay a services fee. He claimed it represented 'a form of compulsory student unionism' and not, as the universities claimed, the only way that they could continue to offer services.

There was also the aforementioned appointment of venerable Liberal warrior Bronwyn Bishop to the role of Speaker of the House, thereby sidestepping the need to put her on the front bench (where the existing female/blonde/person-with-surname-'Bishop' quota was already filled) while also guaranteeing a deeply partisan authority controlling the action in the chamber.

Abbott was excitingly pious in his announcement, declaring, 'I want to bring some dignity back to the parliament and that means a Speaker who can control the parliament and who can act without fear nor favour. And I want someone who is as tough on the government as on the Opposition because I think the people expect a parliament which is a genuine debating chamber and not just a chamber where the government bludgeons the Opposition.'

As a demonstration of this action without fear or favour, it's worth noting that on 27 November 2014, Bishop ejected a record-setting eighteen Labor MPs from the 'genuine debating chamber', thereby bringing her running total of ejected MPs to 285, of which 280 were Labor. So . . . maybe a *little* bit of favour there, perhaps?

In yet more happy news for the government, the PM's chief of staff Peta Credlin had all her drink-driving charges dismissed by the ACT courts. Phew![3]

Then there were cuts. Oh, how there were cuts!

The Climate Change Authority and the independent Climate Commission were immediately defunded on the grounds that there was already a Climate Change portfolio, which had also been eliminated. There was also no sense of irony in the government's decision to let a quarter of the national Centrelink staff use their own services to pursue exciting new employment opportunities elsewhere.

Hockey announced a Commission of Audit to look at what stuff the government had lying around that it might be able to flog off. Medibank Private seemed like an obvious target, as

---

3 Magistrate Maria Doogan found that the charges had been proven—in other words, that Credlin was over the limit and behind the wheel—but decided that she didn't deserve to have a conviction recorded due to the low reading and otherwise clean record. The magistrate just wanted to give a basically good kid a second chance, it would seem.

did Australia Post (although there were some pesky legislative issues to get around for that one). He also somewhat unexpectedly raised the government's debt ceiling from $300 billion to $500 billion, which should have given some indication that perhaps he wasn't quite as worried about the deficit as he would subsequently insist he was. Then again, the fractious United States Congress had not long shut down its government over the exact same issue, so maybe it was just on his mind.

And, of course, there was the carbon tax.

The carbon tax had been the stick used to successfully beat the Gillard government, begetting the popular 'Ju-LIAR' meme as revenge for her having declared that there would be no such levy in any government that she led—which was unfortunate for Gillard since a) it was a solidly positive idea, and b) introducing a price on carbon was a necessary condition of the support of the Greens in her minority government.

The popular idea of the tax placing onerous demands on working Australians was one that, on the face of it, could have been dispensed with quickly and early. For a start it only applied to polluters, not consumers, and while in theory this could have seen some companies choose to up their prices to accommodate the new cost of emissions, most would instead seek to lower their emissions and therefore avoid paying the tax—which was, after all, the entire aim of the scheme. And that's exactly what happened: emissions dropped in the energy sector (though not the high-polluting transport or agriculture sectors, which were exempt from the tax for political reasons), prices didn't skyrocket, investment in the renewable energy sector grew precipitously, and the world failed to end. However, for the Gillard government it was a PR disaster in that its leader had said one thing and then done another, and failed to sell the change in direction to the electorate—or, at least, the bit of the electorate that read the Murdoch-owned press.

Abbott campaigned furiously on the repeal of the carbon tax, painting it as an onerous restriction on industry and a constant burden on taxpayers, who saw their power bills steadily rising. Sure, that rise had nothing to do with the carbon tax—not least because it only kicked in as of 1 July 2012—but Labor either didn't want to get into the nitty-gritty of the numbers, or perhaps didn't want to confess its own culpability in what was actually pushing the prices up: the clumsy, inefficient sweetheart deals that Labor and Liberal state governments had made over the previous two decades as privatisation of state power assets came into vogue.[4]

Abbott had ridden into power on the back of the carbon tax repeal and demanded that the new government be permitted to carry out its mandate as early as possible—although, with the Greens still holding the balance of power in the Senate until July 2014, such repeal required either their support or that of Labor. Neither seemed likely to budge.

As early as October 2013 the PM was flagging a possible double dissolution to break the deadlock if the Opposition didn't agree to pass the repeal before the December break.

---

4   It's too complex and depressing an area to get into here, but one example was the situation in New South Wales where the government guaranteed full reimbursement plus 10 per cent for all upgrades of the technically public-owned 'poles and wires' grid by the private companies that ran them. Unsurprisingly, companies were awfully keen to keep upgrading the systems, even as demand went down. In 2012 NSW power customers coughed up between $30 and $40 million for the Charleston Zone sub-station near Newcastle, despite it reportedly not even being hooked up to the grid.

It was an ambitious plan since the government didn't have a piece of twice-rejected legislation to take before the governor-general as a trigger for such an election and couldn't realistically get one before March 2014 at the earliest, at which point it would have to explain to the nation why it chose to impose an early election over a piece of legislation it could probably have passed a few weeks later—but it did indicate how little interest the government had in waiting to enact its policies, much less negotiating with the non-ruling parties. It also indicated just how early the idea of a double dissolution was on the table as a potential government strategy.

———

Meanwhile, amid the smoke and rubble of the Labor bunker, things were looking grim. For one thing, it now had to come up with a new leader—one who would be a small target for the pugnacious new PM, while being popular enough to sidestep the half-or-more-of-the-party-want-them-gone statistics that plagued Gillard and Rudd.

As Rudd resigned from the leadership and indicated that he would also be leaving parliament, Labor wasted no time in starting the process of selecting its new leader, who everyone correctly predicted would be inner-city Melbourne MP Bill Shorten.

Other names had been thrown around by hopeful progressives, such as that of Sydney's MP Tanya Plibersek, despite her being female and therefore basically Julia Gillard in the eyes of Murdoch-owned press, and popular SA senator Penny Wong, who had the triple strike of being female, openly lesbian and inconveniently stuck in the upper house. Shadow treasurer Chris Bowen was another early contender, but he made it clear that he had no intention of running for the big chair.

The only other serious contender was Plibersek's electoral neighbour, Anthony Albanese. The affable Member for Grayndler had been made interim leader after Rudd's resignation, but had been a vocal supporter of the former PM: a tie which made him a liability with the anti-Rudd electorate. Also, as an outspoken working class chap who never shied away from a verbal sparring match, there was a danger that he wouldn't be the small target that the party felt was needed.

A ballot of the parliamentary party and the rank-and-file membership—the first under the rules specifically introduced by Kevin Rudd when he reclaimed the leadership, which were intended to prevent the sort of leadership destabilisation that had led to his return—saw Shorten narrowly beat Albanese with a slim majority of just over 52 per cent, although Albanese handsomely won the rank-and-file membership vote. The announcement of Plibersek as deputy and Wong as leader in the Senate contrasted strongly with the Coalition's representation of women.[5]

But this drama flared only briefly. Everyone in the party seemed to grasp that from now, all the fights were to happen out of the public eye. Labor had to be unified—or, at the very least, give the impression of unity—if it was to have any hope of returning from the wilderness. And it was a long road back.

---

5 Not that Labor did an especially spectacular job with gender parity itself, mind. Yes, it did put eleven women in the shadow ministry, but nine of them were in junior roles. Former speaker Anna Burke was outspokenly critical of the move, arguing 'there is no meritocracy' in the party ('Yes, I am bitter and disappointed. Once again, Labor failed women', *Guardian*, 14 October 2013).

4
THE RIGHT TO BE A BIGOT

*In which the captain lets an ill-starred crewman navigate
the treacherous Reef of Public Disapproval*

One of the more obvious salvos in the Abbott government's war against what they saw as being the relentless leftism of the culture was an attempt to play up the ever-popular Freedom of Speech card in shouting down dissenting opinion.

It's worth spending a quick moment on the subject of the Special Precious Right to Free Speech, since it's a term that gets thrown around a hell of a lot by people who seem to mistakenly think that it means the Special Precious Right to Say Whatever the Hell You Want in Any Forum and Be Immune from Consequences.

Whenever a politician wants to make a sweeping gener-alisation about dole bludgers, a public commentator wants to explain why Islam scares them, or a hack comedian gets blowback for telling a joke about raping women, you can guarantee that their Right to Free Speech will be loudly and defensively invoked as though it's a thing that clearly and definitively exists.

Technically, of course, the right to free speech in Australia exists only in terms of there being few legislated restrictions on public speech. There's no such 'right' conferred in the Constitution—and even where such rights *do* exist, as with the First Amendment to the United States Constitution, it only operates in terms of the government being specifically prevented from censoring one's speech.

In practice, Australia has fairly robust freedoms when it comes to speech, but it isn't completely unfettered. Defamation law makes it possible to claim damages when people do make false statements about others. Commercial-in-confidence clauses prevent people from disclosing information that might be professionally compromising. Using offensive language in public can get one arrested. Indeed, the government that declared it was all about freedom of speech was perfectly happy to introduce laws limiting protection for journalists and whistle-blowers (and, for that matter, teachers and doctors working in detention centres), to which we shall presently come.

And then there's hate speech, which is covered under the Racial Discrimination Act.

———

The Institute of Public Affairs had made clear in its demands on the government, as outlined in 'Be Like Gough', that one of its particular bugbears was the onerous conditions on free speech imposed by the Racial Vilification Act and specifically the grounds under which the conservative broadcaster, News Corp columnist and staunch Coalition supporter Andrew Bolt was successfully charged in 2011.

Freedom of speech has always been one of the great concerns of the IPA and, by extension, the Liberal Party; although it's a very specific version of freedom of speech—to wit, Freedom of Speech by the Person Who Shouts Loudest. The IPA is certainly not interested in agitating for the freedom for ordinary people to get their speech across, for example: things like media access and diversity are among the things specifically opposed by the organisation, as evidenced by their staunch opposition to media ownership restrictions. Its concern is about the eroding of the right for wealthy, right-wing individuals to rail about entirely imagined threats from non-wealthy and non-right-wing types.

Thus it was no surprise that this would be the particular responsibility of former IPA policy director Tim Wilson, whom Attorney-General George Brandis appointed to the Australian Human Rights Commission in mid-December 2013.

Cynics might have suggested that this was a transparently partisan appointment, given that the AHRC was an organisation that the IPA had publicly demanded be abolished as recently as the previous January. Cynics might have pointed out in addition that Brandis looked a wee bit hypocritical since he'd been loudly critical of the previous Labor government's appointment of ex-Bob Carr staffer Dr Tim Soutphommasane to the position of race discrimination commissioner, castigating the partisan nature of the appointment and declaring that the AHRC had 'become an ideologically driven agency whose agenda lies entirely with advancing the causes of the Left'.

More jaded cynics might even have thought Wilson a Liberal Party mole whose job was to undermine the work of the organisation generally and the outspoken head of the AHRC, Professor Gillian Triggs, in particular, as she had already proved a thorn in the side of the government over offshore processing and the conditions of Australia's detention centres.

But those suggestions would be unfair. Accurate, perhaps, but unfair.

Wilson's appointment also makes sense when considering Abbott's pre-election promises to the IPA—though not the public at large, of course—during his April 2013 speech celebrating the IPA's sixtieth anniversary: 'We will repeal Section 18C of the Racial Discrimination Act, at least in its current form.'

This crusade had a personal element for the IPA beyond its ideological agenda. Aside from Bolt's high-profile support of the organisation and the government it advised, Bolt's son James had a gig as the IPA's communications director.

Thus Brandis had been tasked with the job of ensuring that the repeal took place, and it was largely assumed that it would be a straightforward slam dunk. After all, this was a government that had been voted in, in part, on the back of a virulently xenophobic anti-asylum-seeker platform. Heck, how hard could it be to pass a law making it easier to be openly racist?

———

Before going into the government's urgent passion for reform in the supposed name of freedom of speech, it's worth taking a moment to look carefully at the restrictions and limitations that the Racial Discrimination Act imposes and how often it's actually been used.

First up, in spite of the manner in which it's generally presented as a hand-wringing sop to easily offended cry-babies, the act isn't all about protecting people from hearing things they don't like. In fact, the conditions under which Section 18C applies are remarkably limited.

The Racial Discrimination Act 1975 was introduced by the Whitlam government and was designed mainly to address ridiculous discrimination in Australia over things like access to housing, employment and services. If you just went, 'Hang on, so it was perfectly legal to refuse service to someone on the basis of their race in Australia until freakin' *1975*?', then congratulations: your brain is functioning correctly.

Section 18C concerns itself with racially offensive behaviour, including speech, and 18D outlines exceptions. These were the bits that Brandis wanted to strip, so it's worthwhile reading them in their entirety. They're neither long nor complicated.

RACIAL DISCRIMINATION ACT 1975—SECT 18C
Offensive behaviour because of race, colour or national or ethnic origin

(1) It is unlawful for a person to do an act, otherwise than in private, if:

   (a) the act is reasonably likely, in all the circumstances, to offend, insult, humiliate or intimidate another person or a group of people; and

   (b) the act is done because of the race, colour or national or ethnic origin of the other person or of some or all of the people in the group.

Note: Subsection (1) makes certain acts unlawful. Section 46P of the Australian Human Rights Commission Act 1986 allows people to make complaints to the Australian Human Rights Commission about unlawful acts. However, an unlawful act is not necessarily a criminal offence. Section 26 says that this Act does not make it an offence to do an act that is unlawful because of this Part, unless Part IV expressly says that the act is an offence.

(2) For the purposes of subsection (1), an act is taken not to be done in private if it:

    (a) causes words, sounds, images or writing to be communicated to the public; or

    (b) is done in a public place; or

    (c) is done in the sight or hearing of people who are in a public place.

(3) In this section: 'public place' includes any place to which the public have access as of right or by invitation, whether express or implied and whether or not a charge is made for admission to the place.

RACIAL DISCRIMINATION ACT 1975—SECT 18D
Exemptions

Section 18C does not render unlawful anything said or done reasonably and in good faith:

(a) in the performance, exhibition or distribution of an artistic work; or

(b) in the course of any statement, publication, discussion or debate made or held for any genuine academic, artistic or scientific purpose or any other genuine purpose in the public interest; or

(c) in making or publishing: (i) a fair and accurate report of any event or matter of public interest; or (ii) a fair comment on any event or matter of public interest if the comment is an expression of a genuine belief held by the person making the comment.

As you may be able to surmise from the above, it's fairly difficult to make a case that fulfils the criteria of 18C while avoiding the many, many exemptions of 18D—particularly given somewhat subjective terms like 'fair comment' and 'genuine belief'.

That might explain why so few cases have progressed to the Federal Court, and why complainants so rarely win. In fact, less than 5 per cent of all complaints made under section 18C ever get to court, due to the specificity of the legislation, and of those cases that have successfully come before a judge more than half were then dismissed.

More specifically, there were only seventy-seven cases between 1997 and 2013, of which thirty-two were upheld.

Barely any of those cases dealt with offensive language in the media, which also puts the lie to the popular idea that the legislation stifles the free and open exchange of ideas in the public sphere. Indeed, the overwhelming majority of the cases were to do with sustained and well-documented bullying of non-Caucasian people in the workplace.

In other words, even during the Bolt case in 2011 this wasn't exactly an urgent and dramatic issue; the court wasn't clogged up with mean-spirited cases brought against well-intentioned journalists accidentally running afoul of a repressive piece of legislation while going about their legitimate business. Given the wording of Section 18D, in fact, it's hard to see how any journalist could possibly get stung by 18C while plying their professional craft. Why, they'd have to do something silly—like, say, deliberately attempt to inflame public outrage by misrepresenting a situation with straight-up falsehoods.

Which neatly brings us to what happened to stir up the IPA—and, by extension, the Liberal Party—against the act.

———

In 2009 Andrew Bolt wrote two articles for the Melbourne *Herald Sun* in which he asserted that light-skinned people deliberately claimed Aboriginal heritage in order to benefit from affirmative action-style employment policies and access to grants.

In his column of 15 April titled 'It's so hip to be black', Bolt raved against visual artists Bindi Cole and Annette Sax, authors Tara June Winch and Kim Scott, academic Associate Professor Anita Heiss, former ATSIC head Geoff Clark and politician Pat Eatock, among many others, all of whom had the temerity to claim their (undisputed) Aboriginal ancestry without having the good grace to be so obviously Aboriginal as to have experienced what Bolt apparently considered to be suitable amounts of prejudice.

More specifically, Bolt raged that they were opportunistic in claiming their cultural identity. He was especially indignant about how these people 'chose' to identify as Aboriginal instead of, as he put it, as a 'take-me-as-I-am human being'—a theme to which he returned a few months later in the 21 August *Herald Sun* column cleverly titled 'White fellas in the black', also published under the title 'The new tribe of white blacks'. In this piece he took aim at artist Danie Mellor and academic Mark McMillan for winning Aboriginal-only awards and scholarships, and castigated the insufficient blackness of academic Professor Larissa Behrendt and his old foes Cole, Sax and Winch.

The gist of the articles was that the battling taxpayers were being taken for a ride by these so-called affirmative action do-gooders establishing things like diversity hires and Aboriginal-only grants, since all these Indigenous Australians— who weren't even black enough to be properly discriminated against—were somehow able to access them. Buried in the vitriol was an argument that these benefits were going to well-resourced middle-class folks rather than the underprivileged Indigenous Australians who could perhaps benefit more directly from such opportunities. However, this not-unreasonable discussion point was overshadowed by a detailed (yet, as it turned out, inaccurate) examination of the family trees of various beneficiaries to determine whether they were Aboriginal enough, by Bolt's reckoning, to be eligible to use the term.

He wasn't afraid to throw some homophobia into the mix too, with a swipe at McMillan, 'whose confusion about his identity leads him also to declare he's both a "proud gay" and a "proud father"' while decrying 'people who looked Aboriginal, but [are] as pink in face as they are in politics', just in case you didn't realise that this was all part of a vast left-wing conspiracy to destroy 'the noble ideal of Australia', in which, as he put it, 'We judge each other by our character and deeds, and not our faith, fortune or fatherland . . . We're not yet a nation of tribes, but that's sure the way we're heading . . . people who feel they owe most to their tribe tend to feel they owe less to the rest. At its worst, it's them against us.'

Oddly enough, the specific people being written about—especially Eatock—weren't charmed by this slander and decided to make a complaint, which came before the court in 2011.

That September the Federal Court's Justice Mordecai Bromberg ruled that Bolt's articles were not written in good faith and contained factual errors—which in itself was not perhaps the single most jarring shock the nation's ever experienced—and that the articles would have offended a 'reasonable member of the Aboriginal community'.

In the decision of the court it was never suggested that Bolt should be punished for expressing an unpopular position. The issue was that he made false assertions in order to argue a racially inflammatory case, and this eliminated the 'in good faith' protections of Section 18D. For example, Bolt described two of the men he was accusing of claiming an arbitrary Aboriginal ancestry—Wayne and Graham Atkinson—as 'Aboriginal because their Indian great-grandfather married a part-Aboriginal woman', rather than the more accurate 'all four of their grandparents and both of their parents were Aboriginal'. And while this sort of sloppy journalism wasn't illegal so much as inept, it undermined any claim that Bolt had written the article while 'making or publishing a fair and accurate report . . . or a fair comment'.

Even so, the ruling came as a surprise. Given the evident difficulties in making a case under 18C and 18D, and the deep pockets of the News Ltd legal fund, it seemed far more likely that the court would conclude that the articles were insulting and arguably defamatory to the individuals named, but not technically hate speech. That Bromberg ruled otherwise did nothing to convince Bolt that he wasn't the unfortunate victim of activist judges pushing their insidious left-wing agenda on innocent Australians.

This was 'a terrible day for free speech in this country', he lamented outside of court. 'It is particularly a restriction on the freedom of all Australians to discuss multiculturalism and how people identify themselves. I argued then and I argue now that we should not insist on differences between us but focus instead on what unites us as human beings.'

And thus did a cause find its célèbre.

———

So, against that background, the IPA made clear that this was a cultural battleline.

In case there was any doubt as to how urgent this was in the organisation's mind, 'Repeal Section 18C of the Racial Discrimination Act' was the fourth priority outlined in the 'Be Like Gough' wish list. Abbott had confirmed it was a priority for his government, and thus Brandis knew what he had to do: remove these restrictions, lest they once again punish powerful journalists for expressing inflammatory inaccuracies about people's heritage.

And Brandis evidently was feeling bullish about the changes being passed. He must have been to blithely say something as transparently silly as the phrase that may yet adorn his gravestone, and which marked the end of any hopes to quietly alter the legislation: 'People do have the right to be bigots, you know.'

This deathless phrase was uttered in the Senate on Monday, 24 March 2014, following an increasingly furious argument over changes to a piece of legislation that hadn't yet even been properly outlined, much less introduced, and did more to galvanise opposition to the proposals than any grassroots organisation could have hoped to achieve. The image of Brandis, red-faced and indignant, complaining in parliament about how people were too gosh-darn sensitive about discrimination he never would experience became a potent symbol of the government. It represented a growing sense that the government was not just indifferent to the wellbeing of a good slab of the population, but actively held them in contempt.

Brandis had made clear his intentions, and the motivations behind them, in public statements the previous week. 'It is certainly the intention of the government to remove from the Racial Discrimination Act those provisions that enabled Andrew Bolt to be taken to the Federal Court merely because he expressed an opinion about a social or political matter,' he railed with righteous zeal. 'I will very soon be bringing forward an amendment to the RDA which will ensure that that can never happen in Australia again.'

At this point it wasn't entirely clear exactly what amendments Brandis was proposing, although it later transpired that he sought to at least remove the 'offend, insult, humiliate or intimidate' provisions from the act, leaving it open only to those who could argue that the speech caused direct physical harm. *The Australian* also reported that there was a move to get rid of the 'good faith' provisions that tripped Bolt up, thereby removing any requirement that the statements made in public be factually accurate or not deliberately intended to be offensive.

Predictably, this didn't go down super well with the nation's various ethnic, religious and cultural groups. Less predictable was the speed with which a unique coalition of groups— including the National Congress of Australia's First Peoples, the Armenian National Committee of Australia, the Arab Council Australia, the Chinese Australian Services Society, the Korean Society of Sydney, the Australian Hellenic Council, the Chinese Australian Forum and the Executive

Council of Australian Jewry—united to pen a joint statement making clear their opposition to any such watering down of the law.

And even within the government there were concerns about the message being sent to the community at large, with Liberal National MP Ewen Jones counselling the party that the move looked too transparently ideological and that maybe a bunch of privileged white men weren't the best people to be lecturing a multicultural nation about what is and isn't offensive and discriminatory speech.

'As a middle-aged white man I have never experienced any form of discrimination,' Jones accurately explained to *The Guardian* on 18 March, 'and I think we should be very aware of listening to opinions of people who have experienced it.'

Others in the party were more forthright, such as Indigenous Western Australian MP Ken Wyatt, who openly threatened to cross the floor if the proposal was brought to a vote. Meanwhile, the Greens made clear that any legislative change introduced before July was doomed to be killed in the upper house in any case.

While Abbott insisted that what he sought was consensus, he declared that the changes would be going ahead despite increasingly loud public and private disapproval. Brandis's determination remained undiminished, and it was with the unshakable confidence of righteous victory that he followed up his declaration about the rights of bigots (in response to Indigenous senator Nova Peris's query: 'Won't removing 18C facilitate vilification by bigots?') by saying, 'In this country people have rights to say things that other people find offensive or bigoted. There is no law that prohibits the incitement to racial hatred. When the government deals with this matter the law will be in a better position to deal with incitement to racial hatred.'

His words were no doubt intended as the clarion call for his crusade but, in hindsight, they were actually its death knell. If that statement prepared the grave for the changes, Brandis nailed the coffin shut by next taking aim at Labor's leader in the Senate, the Malaysian-born and openly gay senator Penny Wong: a woman who presumably knew a thing or two about experiencing prejudice in Australia.

When Wong mocked his desire to protect the bigots by rendering Section 18C effectively toothless, Brandis waxed condescending.

'Well you know, Senator Wong, I think a lot of the things I have heard you say in this chamber over the years are, to my way of thinking, extraordinarily bigoted and extraordinarily ignorant but I would defend your right to say things that I find to be bigoted and ignorant. That is what freedom of speech means.'

Despite his stirring language, the public didn't rush to applaud Brandis's magnanimous tolerance of his parliamentary colleague. However, George clearly didn't read the public mood, since the following day he returned to the theme on 2GB, insisting: 'We don't ban free discussion because somebody might be offended by it.'

It was a disingenuous—if predicable—interpretation of the actual legislation, which quite obviously doesn't call for language to be banned simply because somebody was offended. More worrying, though, was the fact that the attorney-general was apparently indicating ignorance of the many, many laws which make very clear that discussion can absolutely be banned *precisely* because people are offended.

Aside from the Racial Discrimination Act, there is the Sex Discrimination Act which outlaws sexual harassment; there are numerous state laws regarding offensive behaviour in public (such as the NSW Summary Offences Act); and many pieces of Criminal Code legislation cover such matters as sending threatening material via the post and making abusive phone calls, all of which limit freedom of speech. But maybe Brandis would have found a way to liberalise them next, had he not been so cruelly thwarted.

Sadly, we were denied any possibility of hearing George potentially declaring that people have the right to threaten rape and murder, because, after all that sound and fury, his legislative changes never even made it to parliament.

By August the government confirmed that it would not be proceeding, with Abbott declaring that petty things like freedom of speech were not as important as unity in the face of terrorism—specifically from the Muslim community.

In his self-described 'leadership call' on 5 August, the PM declared that 'when it comes to counter-terrorism, everyone needs to be part of Team Australia. The government's proposals to change 18C of the Racial Discrimination Act have become a complication in that respect. I don't want to do anything that puts our national unity at risk at this time and so those proposals are now off the table.' At least there was an admission that national unity might be risked later, though, so the IPA could still dream.

Yet Brandis looked glum about the poor bigots whose rights would stay undefended, but at least he could take comfort from the enormously restrictive security laws that the government was hoping to bulldoze through parliament.

There's something in there about collecting people's metadata, he presumably thought. *Should probably look up what metadata actually means, just in case anyone asks. Actually, nah, should be fine.*[1]

The dream of repealing 18C might have been dead for the time being, but it was far from forgotten. After all, someone still needed to be the champion of the bigots.

And in January 2015 Cory Bernardi took the opportunity to use the murder of cartoonists at French satirical magazine *Charlie Hebdo* to thunder righteously for the repeal of Sections 18C and 18D.

'The time for being bullied is over—we cannot negotiate with the intolerant . . . Let's fight for fundamental freedoms and reject those who will pursue aims that are at odds with that.'

Just to clarify: Bernardi was arguing that removing penalties for hate speech would *decrease* intolerance, because . . . um, something.

But no-one particularly minded. After all, if Bernardi made a contradictory statement outlining his own peculiar prejudices in a forest, did it really make a sound?

---

1   Foreshadowing!

5

FOR THOSE WHO'VE COME ACROSS THE SEAS . . .

In which the captain learns some interesting political lessons

One of Abbott's most successful slogans in the lead up to the 2013 election was 'Stop the Boats!', indicating an interesting new development in the Australian psyche. Despite being a country based on immigration, to the point where the national anthem declares, 'For those who've come across the seas / We've boundless plains to share',[1] the people of Australia had looked at the successes of multiculturalism and gone, 'Yeah, sure, this nation was built on the successful interplay of wave after wave of new ideas and energetic people building new lives here, including refugees fleeing persecution from repressive and murderous regimes. But, having said that, fuck 'em.'

---

1   And here's as good a point as any to reconfirm my commitment to replacing 'Advance Australia Fair' with a better anthem: specifically, John Farnham's 'Pressure Down'. You know it's what the Australian republic is waiting for.

It's worth having a look at the roots of this excitingly small-minded new public philosophy, because it's not immediately obvious to see how a nation went from being a leading light in the fight for human rights to becoming an international pariah on the subject.

That's because it wasn't easy. It took a lot of concerted effort.

———

Australia's been tricky on the subject of who exactly should get to live in the country and under what circumstances ever since Joseph Banks determined that Aboriginal people were not sufficiently developed to claim Terra Australis as their own and that the British Crown could pretty much just consider it unoccupied territory.[2]

Despite this inauspicious beginning, we haven't always been terrified of newcomers. On the one hand, we've often been impressively solid on helping folks flee oppression, from Lutherans fleeing Prussia to the safer haven of South Australia in 1839 through to our government-assisted migration program for European Jews in the late 1930s and our endorsement of the establishment of the Office of the United Nations High Commissioner for Refugees in 1950. Then again, there was the whole White Australia policy thing,

---

2 The sealed orders instructing James Cook to set sail to find the theorised Southern Continent specified that claiming of such a place would proceed 'with the Consent of the Natives to take possession of Convenient Situations in the Country in the Name of the King of Great Britain'. Surprisingly—and heartbreak-ingly—it was the humanist Banks, who so celebrated the culture and people (and especially the ladies . . .) of the Polynesian Islands, who decided that no negotiation was required. Just think about what sorts of later genocide could have been averted if Banks had recommended a more diplomatic approach. From little things, big things grow . . .

which began with the Immigration Restriction Act of 1901 (aka the We Just Don't Like Them Chinamen Act) and which we didn't get around to properly eliminating until 1973.

The story of Australia's refugee policy properly begins with the aftermath of World War II, when the former Allies began to sort out the question of what to do about the millions of displaced people in Europe. Australia got enthusiastically on board, welcoming an estimated 170,000 refugees between 1947 and 1953. We maintained that enthusiasm for the next few decades as people fled the Soviet Bloc, particularly Hungary and Czechoslovakia, and later fled dictators like Pinochet in Chile and Idi Amin in Uganda. The war in Vietnam and conflict in Timor saw an influx of refugees from our region, and prompted a change to Australia's somewhat ad hoc approach to arrivals and the development of a more regimented humanitarian settlement program. And with those changes came an increasing amount of restrictions.

The Migration Legislation Amendment Act 1989 made it lawful to arrest those suspected of not being in Australia for legitimate reasons. But the first hint that maybe we were moving less towards helping people and more towards criminalising them was the 1992 passage of the Migration Reform Act by the Labor government of Paul Keating; this act, which came into effect on 1 September 1994, made detention mandatory for everyone who turned up without a visa.

Just in case that seemed like a reasonable sort of measure— you know, to ensure that we knew who was here, whether they were seeking asylum, what their circumstances were—it's worth remembering the stirring words of then-immigration minister

Gerry Hand, who made it clear the act was designed to stop these greedy foreigners (specifically, Vietnamese, Cambodian and Chinese foreigners) coming and taking our stuff: 'The government is determined that a clear signal be sent that migration to Australia may not be achieved by simply arriving in this country and expecting to be allowed into the community,' he declared during the second reading of the bill, although he added 'this legislation is only intended to be an interim measure'.

It's also worth noting that September 1994 was thus the first time that people turning up without a visa were deemed 'unlawful', a theme that was to become rather more pronounced as time went on. Also, significantly, the new laws removed time limits on how long people could be held in detention. Now it was perfectly legal to hold people indefinitely—a situation that was to become increasingly popular.

While Keating was the first PM to criminalise the act of arriving without a visa, it wasn't until the prime ministership of John Howard that Australia really transitioned from 'asylum seekers' to 'criminals'. And that's because being suspicious of foreigners had come back into political vogue.

———

Australia had started to rediscover its taste for xenophobia by the late nineties, despite aggressive anti-Asian sentiment having up to then been confined to the far-right fringes of racist extremists like the virulently stupid National Action.[3]

---

3 Their racism is a matter of public record now too: National Action's somewhat-less-than-charming-and-erudite leader, Michael Brander, attempted to sue Adelaide's Messenger Newspapers for defamation in 1995 when editor Des Ryan wrote a column calling him racist (and also effeminate and a 'juvenile attention-seeker'). The case was dismissed in 1999 on the grounds that this description was a fair comment, and Brander's appeal failed on the same grounds in 2000.

But then, like grunge music before it, racism went unexpectedly mainstream. The crossover artist who made it cool again was Queensland MP Pauline Hanson, first as an independent elected to the House of Representatives for Oxley and then as founder of One Nation.

———

The former fish-and-chip-shop proprietor had been dropped by the LNP for comments about how Aboriginal people were always expecting handouts. She then campaigned as an independent in the Labor-held seat of Oxley and managed a comprehensive swing against the sitting member, Les Scott, in the March 1996 election.

In case there was any doubt about her stance on these delicate matters, her maiden speech to parliament in September that year railed against the 'Aboriginal industry' that was living off the public purse, and included the agenda-setting line: 'I believe we are in danger of being swamped by Asians.'

One Nation was founded the following year by Hanson, former Abbott staffer David Oldfield and David Etteridge, and trumpeted its zero-net immigration policy and an aggressive assertion of Australian culture, defined largely as 'not multiculturalism'. Asylum seekers were most avowedly unwelcome.[4] The party won almost a quarter of the primary vote at the 1998 Queensland election, but this was the party's high-water mark: Hanson lost her seat in that year's federal election

---

4 Among the principles outlined on their website in 1998, 'Compassion must be extended to genuine refugees but temporary refuge need not extend to long-term permanent settlement in Australia.' and 'No person other than an Australian citizen, or a permanent resident of the Australian community, has a basic right to enter Australia.' Of course, compared with current government policy, it still looks positively welcoming.

and the Queensland state party fractured in 1999, with five members defecting to form the stillborn City–Country Alliance, who were entirely wiped out at the polls.

But the popularity of the party, however brief, had not gone unnoticed by John Howard (or, indeed, by Tony Abbott, who even set up a slush fund—the Australians for Honest Politics Trust—with the specific aim of bringing down the One Nation Party). The Howard government had already started to take a hard line on the increasing number of asylum seekers by introducing Temporary Protection Visas (TPVs), which expired after three years and forced holders to reapply or face deportation. However, it wasn't until the Norwegian freighter MV *Tampa* was denied entry to Australian waters in August 2001 that Howard demonstrated just how hard the government's line had become.

The ship had picked up 439 Afghan asylum seekers from a listing vessel on the high seas and attempted to take them to Christmas Island. However, the government refused permission for it to dock, the argument being that, sure, the people rescued at sea were in a vessel in distress, but the *Tampa* itself was not and therefore had no right to expect Australian assistance to offload the people it rescued. This forced a standoff which ended with Australia sending Special Air Service forces to board the vessel.

This in turn led to the hasty passage of the Border Protection Bill that month, which gave the government the power to forcibly prevent any ship or person on board that ship from entering Australian waters, and to deny any claims for asylum being made by those who were on board. Those rescued by the *Tampa* were among the first to be plonked at the shiny new detention centres Australia had built on Nauru and Papua New Guinea as part of what was ominously called 'the Pacific Solution'.[5]

The navy was also tasked with the job of intercepting and turning back asylum boats under the auspices of Operation Relex in 2001. One of those boats, designated Suspected Illegal Entry Vessel (SIEV) X, sank on 19 October as a result of the turnback, drowning an estimated 146 children, 142 women and 65 men. Forty-four people were subsequently rescued from the water, and it transpired that many of the people on the boat had been attempting to reunite with family members in Australia on TPVs.

Now that should have been a PR disaster for the government a mere month out from a federal election—but John Howard finessed it.

The line went like this: the people on SIEV X were not merely being towed, sunk and not-rescued by the Australian navy. No, they had been throwing their children off the ship and into the ocean as a horrific and cold-blooded ploy to get Australia to rescue them. That's what then-immigration minister Philip Ruddock insisted in parliament, with Howard and defence minister Peter Reith backing him all the way, complete with photos of terrified children floundering helplessly in the ocean. The message to the electorate was clear: what sort of monsters were these people? What would they do to our children if they had the chance?

5   How do governments blithely whack 'solution' at the end of policies—especially those that involved the forced relocation of people to prison camps—without someone in their employ going, 'Say, how familiar are you people with German history of the late 1930s? I suspect I might have some very uncomfortable news for you . . .'

Was it accurate? Nope.[6] Did it work? Well, in terms of diffusing an embarrassing situation just ahead of the election, absolutely.

It transpired that one of Reith's advisers, Michael Scrafton, had informed the PM that the information was incorrect even while it was being disseminated to the press and, when uncropped versions of the photos subsequently came to light, it was clear that they were taken *after* the boat sank and that the navy was attempting rescue of people already in the water. The problem with this was the truth came out via a Senate inquiry (largely comprised of non-government senators) held shortly before the 2004 federal election. The timing made it (accurately) seem to be politically motivated rather than illustrating a great hunger for the truth on Labor's part.[7]

In any case, the message for both major parties from the 2001 and 2004 elections was clear: border control is a vote-winner. Also, no-one was going to kick a government out on an issue like their treatment of asylum seekers. This was a lesson carefully learned by all Howard's ministers, and particularly Abbott, and it was to have . . . *consequences.*

———

It's important to point something out at this juncture: the usual narrative has been that the demonisation of asylum seekers

---

6   By 2006 the story had changed slightly, although Howard insisted that he didn't owe an apology to the families whom he claimed had chucked their kids into the sea because 'they irresponsibly sank the damn boat, which put their children in the water'. Ah, of course, they sank it themselves. Why, that just makes sense! (George Megalogenis, 'They sank the boat, Howard says', *Australian*, 27 February 2006.)

7   A Senate Select Committee had previously been established by the Howard government to inquire into the incident in 2002. The inquiry had concluded that there was no evidence to support the claims made by the government, but among other things Scrafton had been instructed by the government that he was not to appear.

made the difference for the languishing Howard government and got it over the line in the election in November 2001. The problem with this narrative, attractive though it appears, is that it's almost certainly wrong. For a start, it's worth remembering that the Coalition won 50.95 per cent of the vote, compared with Labor's 49.05 per cent: a thundering landslide it was not. More importantly, every poll taken at the time suggested that Australians weren't super fussed about the issue of asylum seekers either before or after the *Tampa* or 'Children Overboard'. While border protection was definitely an important issue in the public mind, it was in the context of the threat of terrorism rather than the influx of refugees. That's because something else fairly important happened in September 2001. In the US. On the eleventh. You may remember it yourself.

The evidence would appear to indicate that the al-Qaeda terrorist attacks in the US, and the Howard government's subsequent commitment of Australia to the US-led wars in Afghanistan and Iraq, had a much larger influence than 'illegal arrivals' on the public's demand for strong border policies. One would historically assume a swing to more conservative parties in times of war, and so it proved in this case. The Coalition's border policies were also perceived as being stronger than Labor's, but the issue wasn't considered important enough by the public to swing the result. Indeed, a subsequent analysis of the election concluded: 'If 11 September had occurred but the *Tampa* crisis had not, the Coalition would in all probability still have won the election.'[8]

---

8 Ian McAllister, 'Border protection, the 2001 Australian election and the coalition victory', *Australian Journal of Political Science*, Vol. 38, issue 3, 2003, pp. 445–463.

However, at the time both sides perceived taking a hard line on asylum seekers as more electorally popular than it actually was, with the added benefit that they were a wonderfully soft target. And thus the major parties took the wrong message—that Australia wanted a crackdown on these grasping boat-people types—and ran with it hard.

This misunderstanding was to colour Australia's asylum-seeker policy for the next fifteen years.

6
CLASSIFIED ON-WATER MATTERS

In which the captain's enforcer makes his influence felt

By 2006 the Howard government had expanded the Pacific Solution, building a lovely big new detention centre on the safely-excised-from-the-migration-zone Christmas Island in 2006 to match the Manus Island and Nauru facilities.[1] A report at the time concluded that accommodating each

---

1 Christmas Island had been excised from the migration zone in 2001 after *Tampa*, and was not the only Australian territory from which unauthorised arrivals could no longer claim asylum. Other territories excised from the migration zone included Cocos Island, Ashmore Island, the Cartier Islands and—after the Gillard government changed the zone again in May 2013—Australia. This had the effect of making all migrations under any conditions to be determined entirely at the discretion of the immigration minister, but presumably any asylum seeker who made it to the Australian Antarctic Territory had a procedurally easier run at it. You'll probably want to bring a jumper.

offshore detainee cost $500,000, seven times what deten-
tion in Australia would cost.[2]

The point that is loudly trumpeted by one side of politics,
and sulkily ignored by the other, is that the Pacific Solution
achieved its aim of stopping boat arrivals in Australia. It did
so by brutally stripping people of their rights and imprisoning
them indefinitely in island prison camps, sure, but according
to the terms that the government set itself the brutal means
justified the unpleasant ends.

The change of government in 2007, however, heralded a
change in approach to the question of asylum seekers. The
government of Kevin Rudd scrapped the Pacific Solution
to initial public acclaim and the focus changed to disrupt-
ing regional people-smuggling operations. The last Nauru
detainees were removed in February 2008 and brought to the
mainland. Of course, this did require reopening a few shut-
tered Australian camps, including the notorious and remote
Curtin Immigration Detention Centre in Western Australia.
Temporary Protection Visas were also abolished, as was the
policy of charging detainees for their time in detention.

However, this was accompanied by a dramatic increase in
boat arrivals, which made Rudd look weak on border security—
a point not lost on the Coalition. The Abbott-led Opposition
successfully used this fact as a stick with which to beat the government—and the moral high ground was claimed by declaring

---

2   These figures were quoted in 'A Price Too High', a study by Oxfam and A Just
Australia in which it was pointed out that just about everything required to run
the offshore detention centres had to be shipped or flown in from Australia, from
medical supplies to staff to generators to stationery to (in some cases) drinking
water. These prices were soon to look like a freakin' bargain.

that offshore detention was all about stopping deaths at sea. It was one of the many issues at play when Rudd chose to resign as leader in the face of a challenge by his deputy, Julia Gillard.

As border protection had been identified as an area in which Labor was considered weak, Gillard brought in a suite of exciting new plans to show it was tough on boats, including introducing new 'enhanced' on-water screening procedures for those seeking asylum. The descriptor 'enhanced' was considered to be more positive-sounding than more accurate alternatives, such as 'streamlined', or 'perfunctory', or 'barely-actually-screening'. At the same time, Gillard also sought to build a regional strategy to address displaced people, negotiating another of the popular 'Solution' solutions. This time the focus was Malaysia.

Gillard had put an expert panel together in June 2012, chaired by Air Chief Marshal Sir Angus Houston, to find an acceptable alternative that balanced political expediency ('stopping the boats') with Australia's human rights obligations. The panel recommended that Australia trade unauthorised arrivals languishing in onshore detention centres with already processed refugees in camps in Malaysia. But the plan was slammed from all sides: refugee advocates argued that since Malaysia was not a safe place this would breach Australia's non-refoulement obligations,[3] while shadow immigration minister Scott Morrison berated the government for

---

3 'Refoulement' is the act of sending people to places where there is an established probability that they will face persecution. In later years, this was got around by increasing 'probability' to 'certainty'—stopping just short of requiring a refugee to present a signed letter from a would-be persecutor outlining their planned persecution—before being ignored altogether. By 2014 Iraqi asylum seekers were being blithely returned to a country in which Australian forces were engaged in war with Islamic State, despite Australian officials being unable to accompany them for safety reasons.

even considering sending people to a country that was not a signatory to the United Nations Refugees Convention.[4]

Gillard was determined to force the policy through, but a High Court challenge scuttled it in August 2011, leaving Gillard with few options save a humiliating retreat on the previous closures: Manus Island processing centre was promptly reopened in November, with Nauru following suit in August 2012. Not that these were technically okay either: the United Nations High Commissioner for Refugees inspected both facilities in 2012 and deemed them inadequate and in breach of Australia's human rights obligations, but that wasn't enough to affect the government's new-found zeal for reform. At least, not with an election on the horizon, Labor in internal disarray, and Abbott breathing down their necks.

By the time Rudd was back in power in 2013 his opinion on asylum seekers had hardened significantly. He promised that those found to be legitimate refugees would still not be settled in Australia, but would instead be given the opportunity to make a new life in beautiful Papua New Guinea. This exciting news was followed by a protest in the Nauru facility that escalated to a riot.

And then there was the election.

———

With Scott Morrison taking up the Immigration and Border Control portfolio, as expected, in the new government, things

---

4 The most recent signatory was, conveniently enough, Nauru in June 2011. Yes, this means that the Howard government, of which Morrison was a member, was perfectly okay with sending people to non-signatory countries, but that's the least of the apparent contradictions between S-Moz's deep concern for the rights of asylum seekers during the Labor years and his policies and actions once he got the gig himself.

started to speed up significantly. Already in September he was investigating how to get around Australia's obligations not to send people back to countries where they were known to be in danger—that same refoulement thing about which he was so gosh-darn concerned eighteen months earlier.

And he faced little opposition. Labor, for its part, was also rattling the asylum-seeker cage. Even while it was tussling over the leadership, both Bill Shorten and Anthony Albanese made clear that they were all about Stopping the Boats (because of the deaths at sea and the evil people smugglers, naturally). Bill Shorten declared that 'Desperate people often take desperate measures when seeking security, protection and asylum. It is the people smugglers, not the asylum seekers, who should be persecuted for plying this miserable and dangerous trade.' Because, y'know, asylum seekers have *so* many options!

Operation Sovereign Borders came into effect on 18 September, turning the issue into a military one with all the accompanying military security classifications. Morrison initially took to appearing at his regular media briefings flanked by the operation's commander, Lieutenant General Angus Campbell. However, that openness didn't last long: what was to be the last media briefing was on 20 December, and in mid-January 2014 Morrison announced that he would no longer be briefing media unless 'we have something to say and when we have something to report'.[5]

At the same time the government attempted (and failed) to bring back Temporary Protection Visas. When the Senate

---

5 Among the things neither said nor reported in that statement was that Christmas Island detainees had sewn their lips together as part of an ongoing hunger strike in the centre.

blocked the move, Morrison acted swiftly to make all boat arrivals, regardless of their circumstances, ineligible for protection visas.

While the public may not have been especially opposed to asylum seekers, supporting them was definitely not a popular public stance to take. South Australian Greens senator Sarah Hanson-Young was a consistently outspoken advocate for better treatment of detainees before, during and after the 2013 federal election, and was rewarded by being returned to the Senate by only a thin margin of preferences.

In September SHY, as she was nicknamed, was publicly demanding information on the status of boats known to be pursued by the navy, which Morrison had started deeming 'classified on-water matters', and in December 2013 she went to Nauru to inspect the conditions of the detention centre for herself.[6]

———

The greatest issue for those in detention was the uncertainty. The uncomfortable fact that Australia was legally obligated to accept refugees who met the necessary criteria was largely got around by suspending the processing of detainees' claims for asylum. The upshot was that thousands of people had no idea when—and, increasingly, if—they would ever be released.

This unrest had already curdled into violent riots in Darwin and Nauru, and staff had been briefly and mysteriously evacuated from the Manus Island detention facility in

---

6 Later, during the June 2015 Senate Estimates, it was revealed that she had had some special friends looking out for her; the staff of Wilson Security had carried out covert surveillance on her during her entire stay. Her codename was 'Raven', presumably because the staff at Wilson were all keen fans of Edgar Allan Poe.

early February 2013. Later in the year, things were clearly reaching a tipping point.

And then Scott Morrison decided to put their minds at rest during a visit to Manus Island in late September by personally explaining to the detainees what was going to happen to them, because sometimes all people need is for a figure of authority to come in and confirm that their applications for asylum are no longer being processed. At least, presumably that's what Morrison thought when he chose to tell the detainees on Manus Island that they would never be settled in Australia, that there was 'no third option' and so they could either remain in the camp or go back to where they had come from.

Unsurprisingly, this went down very, very badly—as was to become clear in the subsequent months of inquiries.

Protests escalated on Manus Island as people sought to express their unhappiness at being given the option of either returning to the tender mercies of the country from which they had fled without permission or rotting in the camp until they died. While there were hunger strikes and sit-ins, the protests largely took the form of chanting; and that was what the detainees were doing on 17 February 2014, when the camp called in the PNG police.

This move appeared to provoke the detainees rather than soothe them. The threatening presence of police dog squads didn't help—and neither did the police decision to station two Incident Response Teams at the centre in case things got hairy.

It's worth clarifying exactly what is meant by 'Incident Response Teams' in this context, because the term evokes images of highly trained professional peacekeepers ready to restore order; a more accurate description would be 'police-sanctioned militias of tooled-up locals itching to give them illegals a hiding'.

Despite later insisting that what eventually happened was completely unpredictable, the camp management clearly knew things were about to get real because it evacuated all non-essential staff from the centre as protesting detainees continued to chant. However, by 5.15 pm the protesting had stopped, and things seemed like they might return to some degree of calm. However, the camp's security contractors, G4S, didn't feel that the mere fact that people had shut up was a strong enough reason not to send in teams to shut them up, calling its own off-duty IRT to gather at Hardstand 1 Accommodation. Thus provoked, the chanting began anew.

From here it appears as though a serious of bad decisions and unfortunate circumstances conspired to create a disaster. At 6.19 pm G4S guards were seen speaking to detainees at Oscar compound, and ten minutes later power went off in the Mike compound. This failed to quell the unrest.

The first sign that things were about to get messy was when G4S guards noticed PNG police and their aforementioned IRTs gathering along the centre's evacuation path at 6.45 pm. The lights in Mike compound were restored at 6.49 pm (the power outage seems to have been a not-uncommon failure of the generators rather than some sort of strategy), but tensions were high and guards overseeing Oscar and Foxtrot compounds were calling for action.

At 7 pm an official request was made for the police to enter the centre. According to the G4S log, at 7.10 pm a guard overheard locals insisting that 'no expat Australian or New Zealander will tell us what to do on our land'[7] and that anyone who passed the fence line was fair game. At 7.30 pm all local staff were evacuated from Mike compound after jeers and whistles from detainees. At 7.45 pm G4S reported everything had settled down again. And then, at 8.30 pm, detainees were told that dinner would be late.

Delays in food deliveries were so common that it didn't occur to anyone that this might exacerbate an already-tense situation, to the degree that G4S was planning on changing shifts as per usual, and standing the mobile unit down.

Mike compound's generator went down again at 9.15 pm, and guards started expressing concerns that detainees in Oscar compound were putting on their shoes. They also reported that there was a plan brewing to breach Oscar's fence into Mike. At 9.45 pm, the police were given the go-ahead to enter, and that's when things went to hell.

A war between armed police and unarmed prisoners was only ever going to end one way, but no-one was taking any chances. Detainees pelted the police and dogs with rocks, breached the internal fences between the compounds, and attempted to make a break for freedom via the processing centre, where G4S staff held them off. And then the PNG police opened fire.

In order to determine how aware Morrison was of the situation, you must decide for yourself who is the more

---

7 'Expat'? Surely an expletive would have worked better here.

trustworthy source: Scott Morrison at the time, who claimed that PNG police had opened fire, or Scott Morrison a little later, who claimed that he had no idea what you were talking about. Assuming it's the former, there's the original press release in which Morrison reported: 'Just after 11.20 pm local time PNG police were reported to have fired shots.' The statement has since been deleted from the departmental server.[8]

Ten minutes later the local IRTs claimed they were confronted by violent detainees outside Mike compound, and that's when G4S conceded they'd lost control of the situation. According to G4S logs, there were 'thirty or forty' injured detainees being treated for gunshot wounds and head injuries in a makeshift hospital in the staff accommodation. One of them was a twenty-three-year-old Iranian man named Reza Barati, whose skull had been bashed in with a lump of wood. He was to be the centre's first murder victim.

By 1 am negotiations between the asylum seekers and G4S had begun, and calm was restored. At 2 am detainees were being moved back into the compounds, although Mike had suffered a lot of damage.

As dawn broke in Australia, Morrison made another statement, this time declaring that PNG police had not entered the centre and that, while an asylum seeker had been killed, it had happened outside the compound, where it was not Australia's responsibility. The tune had changed a little by

---

8 The web address is http://www.minister.immi.gov.au/media/sm/2014/sm 211891.htm, if you'd like to plonk it in the Wayback Machine or your internet archive server of choice. You're welcome.

the afternoon, though, with Morrison admitting he wasn't entirely sure where Barati had been killed.[9]

And that's when Morrison's most important job really began: ensuring that absolutely no-one from Australia had been at fault.

---

9 Again, the press release has been expunged from the departmental server but exists on the immortal internet. The relevant quote is: 'In terms of the man who died, he had a head injury and at this stage it is not possible to give any further detail on that, including now, based on subsequent reports, where this may have taken place.'

7
PUTTING THE COAL INTO COALITION

In which the ship's naturalist examines how much poison is beneficial to Australian creatures

One of the few things that came as no surprise with regards to the Abbott government was its environmental policy. Specifically, that said policy would involve a lot of mining.

While many of the promises made before the election playfully changed as soon as the government took its place in Canberra, one policy platform had been clear: 'Climate change is balls and we won't be pandering to it any further.'

The carbon tax would be eliminated, emissions trading halted, the Minerals Resource Rent Tax—which, after all, took money from hardworking and largely foreign companies and gave it back to Australians as though they had some right to the ground beneath their feet—was also removed. The Climate Change Authority was to be defunded, and there were plans to eliminate the Renewable Energy

Target, the Clean Energy Finance Corporation and the Climate Commission.

The man given the job of doing all of this was 'environment' minister Greg Hunt, who had actually done his university thesis on market-based solutions to the problem of greenhouse gas emissions in 1990. *A Tax to Make the Polluter Pay* was co-authored by Hunt and fellow student Rufus Black for their Bachelor of Laws; it won a university prize for best final-year thesis. The premise of their thesis was that the most cost-effective way to reduce emissions would be to tax the amount of pollution created, thereby establishing a strong and immediate incentive for an industry (such as, say, power generation) to reduce their emissions. As Hunt and Black put it in their thesis: 'Ultimately it is by harnessing the natural economic forces which drive society that the pollution tax offers us an opportunity to exert greater control over our environment.'

In other words, if you want to reduce carbon dioxide—to pull this greenhouse pollutant quite literally out of the air— you might calculate how many tonnes of carbon is liberated through the burning of coal, and then impose a 'tax' on the 'carbon'. You can see how this notion might be at odds with the party for which he was elected.

Hunt is by no means a fool: he won a Fulbright Scholarship and studied at Yale, travelled extensively around the world, worked for the UN and was raised by a Victorian Liberal MP father who was characterised as a 'keen environmentalist'. This made him an ideal candidate for the job: a man who didn't deny climate change and who actually understood not just the science of it, but also the economics—and was also a dyed-in-the-wool Liberal. While other Coalition MPs (and the prime minister himself) were on the record scoffing about climate change being part of some shadowy left-wing environmentalist conspiracy, Hunt was genuinely across the issue. The weird thing, then, is that he must also have been aware that in implementing the aforementioned Coalition policy, he was not just doing pointless busy work but also harming the future of life on the planet.

But, fortunately for the government, Hunt was evidently cool with that.

And when he took his place in the Abbott ministry, Hunt had a plan in place. It was clear. It was bold. And, unlike the carbon tax or emissions trading, it wasn't going to put onerous obligations on industry by making them change anything they were doing. Hunt's was a 'direct action' plan: an environmental policy that is distinguished by being neither active nor direct.

———

It's worth taking a moment to explain what direct action is. It's quite straightforward: instead of charging people for polluting, you bribe them not to do so.

These bribes work in a reverse-auction system: a company explains to the government how it will reduce its emissions, the government challenges other companies to do it cheaper, and the one that claims it can do it the cheapest wins the bribe.

You might notice that this doesn't necessarily oblige the other companies to implement their unsuccessful ideas, or indeed to lift a finger to change their policies if they don't fancy doing so. But presumably they get so excited about their emissions reduction plan that they just buckle down and do it anyway out of the goodness of their hearts. Or maybe the satisfaction of competing with other businesses for government bribes is the *real* emissions reduction after all?

A bigger problem with the system was the difficulty in distinguishing between what was an actual new innovation to reduce emissions and what was simply an inevitable consequence of new technologies. Many industries were moving towards lower emissions in any case, simply as technology improved—especially in manufacturing. While fining people for pollution would incentivise swapping over to new technologies sooner rather than later, direct action encouraged a rather more languorous rate of change. After all, industries would be paid regardless—so why rush it? Hence, there's the added wrinkle that a bribe-heavy system worked as a disincentive to early adoption.

There was also something of a PR issue, because an assessment of the effect of the carbon tax and emissions trading scheme revealed that it had been much more successful than even the most optimistic predictions.

In December 2014—specifically, two days before Christmas 2014—Hunt's department quietly released the Australian National Greenhouse Gas Inventory data, which showed that Australia's greenhouse gas emissions had dropped by 1.4 per cent—the largest drop ever—between July 2013 and June 2014; in other words, during the second and final year of the carbon tax.

A departmental spokesthing insisted that there was nothing significant about releasing the embarrassing data just before

Christmas, almost as though it was deliberately trying to bury it and that it released the data at the same time every year. That was technically true, in that it had released the previous year's data—showing a similarly embarrassing drop of 0.8 per cent in emissions,[1] again thanks to the carbon tax—at around the same time. Prior to that, the data had been released in October—but that, obviously, had been under a different government.

You might also think that direct action could be an open-ended fund with which industries could in effect blackmail the government—they might threaten to return to their previous high-emission ways unless they received payments for not polluting. The government got around that potential problem very neatly, though: Abbott simply declared that the fund would never be topped up. Once its budgeted $2.55 billion ran out, it would not be replaced. You can't extort the fund if there's nothing to extort, right?

Of course, it also becomes harder to bribe someone when there is nothing left in the kitty.

It might appear as though the government itself was determined to ensure that direct action would be hamstrung from achieving the modest aims it was purportedly designed to achieve. But that would be cynical.[2]

Depending on which source you accept, the direct action plan is either a genuine, heartfelt attempt to induce companies to reduce their emissions, or a deliberate boondoggle designed to accomplish the flimsiest government action possible on climate change.

---

1   Technically, that number was only 57 per cent as embarrassing.
2   And we can't have THAT!

Arguing for the first of these positions is Hunt himself. In his 2011 Lowy Institute speech 'Carrots not Sticks: Rethinking Global Approaches to Climate Change', he outlined what was to become the direct action plan and argued that paying polluters not to pollute was a more efficient system than charging them every time they did.

In the other corner is basically everybody else, including the scientists and economists who argue the system provides inadequate rewards for industries to bother reducing their emissions, and that the current information regarding the scheme is remarkably unclear about what, if any, criteria or monitoring will take place to ensure that emissions are indeed reduced beyond what one might expect given changes in technology.

There's also John Howard, who, in his address to the Global Warming Policy Foundation in London in November 2013, merrily confirmed that he still didn't buy this 'climate change' nonsense and that direct action was a fig leaf.[3]

As Howard tells it, while the Coalition did set up a task force to address climate change under his watch, it did so with the express purpose of being seen to be doing something without actually being obliged to do anything so grubby as implementing an emissions trading scheme. At least, not until the rest of the world did it first—especially China and Indonesia.

---

3   You're probably doing a double take at the very idea of Howard speaking at such an event, but I should make clear that the Global Warming Policy Foundation is a UK think tank dedicated to preventing any action on climate change, essentially on the demonstrably wrong grounds that it's too expensive and that the science isn't in yet. It gets very righteously indignant when people call it 'denialists', though—in the exact same way that people get righteously indignant when they're called 'racists' just because they discriminate against people on the basis of their ethnicity.

'To put it bluntly, "doing something" about global warming gathered strong political momentum in Australia,' he explained. 'A joint business/government taskforce recommended an ETS, but one that protected our export-exposed sector, including the mining industry. As well, the government indicated that Australia would support a new agreement to limit the growth of greenhouse gas emissions, provided that it bound all emitters. We remained opposed to ratifying the existing Kyoto Protocol.'

The party remained ostensibly in favour of this toothless emissions trading scheme until Abbott became leader of the party, at which point he made clear that there was zero bipartisan support for any such policy, including the one that the Rudd government had been hoping to establish.

Abbott had memorably described climate science as 'absolute crap' in 2009, and by 2010 he was back-pedalling wildly away from the previous consensus on climate science.

———

By mid-2015 Hunt was optimistically claiming that achieving the target of a 5 per cent drop in emissions below the levels of 2000 had become easier, thanks to the closure of such high-emitting culprits as car manufacturers, thereby putting a somewhat hopeful spin on the death of a high-employing industry.

However, the real battleground was over mining—and, in a symbolic twist, one of the major sites was Queensland's Abbot Point.

Adani's massive Carmichael thermal coalmine had been approved for the Galilee Basin, but it had always faced many critical financing issues.[4] The steady decline in the price of thermal coal, particularly as China faced its own economic downturn and world stockpiles of coal increased, made the enormous project seem economically suicidal. Indeed, the Queensland government's own internal assessment was that the mine was 'unbankable'.

However, while most of the planet's big investment banks had declined to put money towards it,[5] new Labor premier Annastacia Palaszczuk supported it, because minority leaders in Queensland do *not* start fights with the mining industry.

Of course, once you've built the cripplingly expensive mine and extracted the increasingly less-valuable coal, there's the question of how you get it out to your shrinking customer base. And that was the biggest problem of all because, to do that, the existing facilities at Abbot Point required comprehensive expansion.

Abbot Point is near Bowen, south of Townsville and north of Mackay, putting it right slap-bang in the middle of the Great Barrier Reef Marine Park. There had been a lot of question marks around the early environmental approval process—specifically, there had barely been any. The federal government had devolved the process to the state government of Campbell Newman, who had pretty much left it to the industry to decide. Oddly enough, their thought was 'yep!'

---

4   The size of said mine was colourfully described by Greenpeace's Ben Pearson as 'seven times that of Sydney Harbour'. Perhaps ironically, that calculation doesn't include the actual harbour at Abbot Point. http://www.abc.net.au/environment/articles/2014/07/28/4025069.htm

5   Deutsche Bank, Barclays, Goldman Sachs and other major concerns backed out of the investment, citing economic, environmental and political concerns with the mine, as did Australian players including, very publicly, the Commonwealth Bank.

In December 2013 Hunt announced that he'd given approval for the $3 billion-dollar expansion of Abbot Point T2 Coal Terminal, including the dumping of three million cubic metres of dredging spoil into the marine park itself.[6] Environmentalists were immediately up in arms, pointing out that this would put fisheries at risk (especially with the silt affecting sunlight to the sea floor, which would affect the growth of seagrasses that were at the bottom of the food chain). Since it's impossible to reach the terminal from the sea without travelling through the reef, increasing the port's capacity would inevitably mean more shipping traffic.

Hunt angrily countered that a number of environmental conditions were included in the approval, but his assurances were not welcomed by those with experience in Queensland environmental politics. This proved prescient given what was to be discovered when the Mackay Conservation Group actually went through the paperwork and . . . actually, we'll come to that in a bit.

One problem cited with the conditions imposed regarding the mine—including an edict that Adani be obliged to monitor water quality for 'up to five years' after the dumping—were somewhat less than stringent. The other, more important issue was that these sort of conditions were routinely ignored by resource and construction companies, not least because the Commonwealth-funded Great Barrier Reef Marine Park

---

6 Fun fact: The Campbell Newman government signed off on the rail link from the Galilee Basin to Abbot Point in December 2013. However, this track had been previously rejected in 2012 and that snub to Clive Palmer's mineral concerns had given him the impetus to angrily quit the LNP and form his own political party. From little things . . .

Authority had very limited powers or resources with which to deal with breaches.

Here's one compelling case study. Clive Palmer-owned Queensland Nickel had illegally dumped polluted water into the marine park on at least two occasions and held concentrated toxic waste in inadequate dams that could potentially leak poisonous waste in the all-but-certain event of a cyclone.[7] In the face of this powerful threat to the environment, the GBRMPA announced that . . . um, it would really rather Palmer didn't do that, if that was okay—not least because it could do nothing to stop him. In a statement the authority wrote: 'We have strongly encouraged the company to investigate options that do not entail releasing the material to the environment and to develop a management plan to eliminate this potential hazard.' But, it explained, this was really down to the company and the state government as 'GBRMPA does not have legislative control over how the Yabulu tailings dam is managed'.

Palmer responded by immediately consulting scientists to find methods by whi . . . nah, just kidding. He threatened to sue the authority for $6.4 billion for being 'obstructionist' if it continued to pretend it had authority over the company's activities in the marine park.[8]

In a completely unrelated development, the federal government reduced its funding of the GBRMPA by $2.8 million

---

7   The company argued at the time that the discharges were necessary in the face of cyclones Hamish in 2009 and Yasi in 2011, although these explanations were not deemed credible by the GBRMPA.

8   Another fun fact: The GBRMPA's entire budget is less than $5 million, so you can understand that it might be a little wary of embarking upon multi-billion dollar lawsuits.

and forced an internal restructure. In any case, no charges were ever laid against Queensland Nickel.

———

Approving major mining projects was just one piece of the puzzle; the government still needed to get rid of the renewable energy sector.

The first priority was the Renewable Energy Target, which had already survived an attempt on its life. Now a new deal was agreed to in May 2015—eventually accepted by Labor— with a reduced target of 33,000 gigawatt hours generated by renewable sources, down from the previous target of 41,000 gigawatt hours. The government also, in an insulting last-minute twist, insisted that the RET should include the high-emission burning of waste wood as a 'renewable' source, presumably because they believe that wood magically reconstitutes when set on fire.

All of this made international renewable energy companies deeply wary of investing in Australia. But at least there was an option for Australian companies: the Clean Energy Finance Corporation.

Attempts to abolish the CEFC had failed in 2014, when Palmer United successfully blocked the legislation, so in July 2015 the government came up with an alternative scheme that didn't require legislation: adding new regulations to the body around what it could and could not invest in. In the 'no' box: wind farms, and household and business solar projects.[9] The new focus would be on 'emerging technologies'—such

———

9   The draft regulation specified that 'mature and established clean energy technologies . . . to be excluded from the corporation's activities, including extant wind technology and household and small-scale solar'.

as . . . um . . . presumably any exciting new energy-generation technique which was promising enough to pass the CEFC's criteria for profitable investment but not so promising that it might actually pose a threat—actual or existential—to the coal industry. The fund announced plans to mount a legal challenge regarding the legitimacy of the new regulations, but the battle was already largely lost.

In October 2014 the prime minister had declared that 'coal is good for humanity, coal is good for prosperity . . . and coal is the world's principal energy source and will be for many decades to come'. People laughed at the time, but now the government had its chance to enforce its rhetoric on reality by making it very clear to the public and the private sector alike that, whatever the science said, investment in renewable energy in Australia was an unreliable and uncertain process.

Just in case that point wasn't quite explicit enough, there was also the charming sight of Abbott's top business adviser Maurice Newman—chair of the PM's business advisory council—frothing in *The Australian* newspaper about how climate change is actually a sinister conspiracy created by the United Nations as part of its 'new world order' agenda.

'This is not about facts or logic,' he said, before leaping into a statement that appropriately contained neither. 'It's about a new world order under the control of the UN. It is opposed to capitalism and freedom and has made environmental catastrophism a household topic to achieve its objective.'[10]

---

10 I encourage you to read the entire lunatic screed at *The Australian*, because it's important to get an idea of the sort of clear-headed acumen that Abbott respects ('The UN is using climate change as a tool not an issue', 8 May 2015).

And the precise degree to which the government was prepared to help out the coal industry was made gloriously clear in June 2015 as the Shenhua Watermark coalmine was given provisional approval to create a massive open-cut project in the Liverpool Plains region of New South Wales, one of the country's most verdant farming regions.

There had been vocal and organised opposition to the plan in the largely agricultural community, but what made the decision especially bitter was that the MP for New England, where the mine was to be built, was one Barnaby Joyce— government frontbencher and, more specifically, Minister for Agriculture.

This particular blow came at an inopportune time for Joyce, since he'd just been all over the international news by declaring that Australia had to avoid marriage equality lest our Asian neighbours stop buying our beef exports—an argument that might not have made a lick of sense (especially as it occurred immediately after the US Supreme Court ratified same-sex marriage and zero Asian countries announced boycotts of their produce), but at least had the good grace to be excitingly original.

Joyce made his displeasure clear in a Facebook post. 'I've never supported the Shenhua [Watermark] mine. I think it is ridiculous that you would have a major mine in the midst of Australia's best agricultural land . . . I've done everything in my power to try and stop the mine . . . I think the world has gone mad when apparently you cannot build a house at Moore Creek because of White Box grassy woodlands but you can build a super mine in the middle of the Breeza plains.'

Oddly enough, his constituents didn't rally around him, making the not-unreasonable point that if the MP and minister was unable to stop a deeply unpopular mine in the middle of their electorate, why exactly had they elected him?

If that wasn't bad enough for ol' Barn, his predecessor—the wildly popular independent MP Tony Windsor—indicated that Joyce's lousy handling of local matters had potentially inspired him to come out of retirement, telling the ABC: 'The approval of the Shenhua mine yesterday was definitely a tick in the positive box in a sense that I'd reconsider [re-entering politics].'

However, a bigger problem came to light in August as the Adani Carmichael mine's environmental approval was over-turned by the Federal Court, courtesy of a challenge by the Mackay Conservation Group (MCG). Unlike the federal minister for the environment, the MCG had actually gone over the paperwork and successfully made the case that the process of approval had not been followed, specifically with regards to greenhouse gas emissions and the effect of the project on two vulnerable species: the yakka skink and the ornamental snake.

The government insisted that this was merely a matter of resubmitting the amended paperwork and that it would be a matter of weeks before things were back on track, but this new controversy promised to do little to attract investment to the still-unfinanced development.

Perhaps that was why the Attorney-General announced plans to make it illegal. 'The government has decided to protect Australian jobs by removing from the Environment

Protection and Biodiversity Conservation Act 1999 [EPBC Act] the provision that allows radical green activists to engage in vigilante litigation to stop important economic projects,' George Brandis announced, even as Labor, the Greens and the majority of crossbench senators confirmed that any such law would be slapped down in the upper house.

Didn't they know about how good coal is? Oh, the *humanity!*

8
NO CUTS TO HEALTH

In which the ship's doctor proves less than able

Traditionally healthcare has always been seen as an area in which the Coalition is weak, principally because it considers health a massive and ongoing drain on the public purse. Its response, indeed its universal panacea to most problems, has historically been a simple solution: 'privatise everything'.

Private healthcare is an area racked with challenges, not least because profiteering from people's suffering seems, at best, to be inexcusably evil. Worse, private ownership fails to make healthcare any cheaper, as the US has learned over the years to its considerable cost—to the point where Barack Obama's administration finally created a public health insurance option in lieu of the type of far-cheaper universal healthcare system that was politically impossible for him to create.[1]

---

1   While Obamacare was a huge step, it's worth pointing out that the idea that for-profit healthcare is inherently disastrous was well entrenched in the public consciousness. After all, one of the most successful television series of the era was based on the distinctly social-justicey premise that a man with a solid, reliable middle-class teaching job, with benefits and security, still couldn't possibly treat his cancer without bankrupting his family—unless he started dealing methamphetamine. (In a related point, who wants to discuss the final episodes of *Breaking Bad*? I have a *lot* of theories.)

Hence it was a difficult time in Australian politics to make a case that maybe the public has had it a bit too good for too gosh-darn long with that healthcare system its taxes have paid for. To make such a case would take a master operator, someone with quick wits and a comprehensive knowledge of the issues, a master orator who could sell the idea of user-pays to an electorate which regarded universal healthcare as both a birthright and a necessary condition for a compassionate society.

Thus it was something of a surprise that this important portfolio was put under the purview of Peter Dutton, a man who wasn't about to slow the government's progress in the area with any of that complicated 'consultation with stakeholders' nonsense.

———

As the Abbott government's health minister, Dutton was given the job of reducing the terrible, terrible drain on the public purse that came from Medicare, and specifically the drain that came from rebates to general practitioners.

Historically public health has suffered from its weird position of being shared between the state and federal governments. Initially it was the sole responsibility of the states, but the introduction of the Pharmaceutical Benefits Scheme made it a federal concern, consolidated by the creation of Medibank and its successor, Medicare. Also, these initiatives were the creations of Labor governments—the PBS was established under PM Ben Chifley in 1948, while Medibank was a Whitlam-era creation—and hence, as far as the Abbott government was concerned, they were clearly ideologically suspect.

The idea behind the PBS was to provide, in the words of

the Act that established it, 'life-saving and disease-preventing drugs' free of charge to Australians who required them. It was an extension of a similar Repatriation Pharmaceutical Benefits Scheme established in 1919 for Australian servicemen and women who had served in the Boer War and World War I. There were several amendments to the scheme in subsequent decades, principally in limiting the number of drugs available (the Liberal-Country coalition government of Robert Menzies reduced the number to 139 drugs, and changed the system to subsidised medicines rather than free ones in 1960), but the general philosophy—that the government would act as the purchasing agent for commonly required medications, buying them in great volume and thus at a lower cost than would otherwise be possible—has remained unchanged since the passage of the Pharmaceutical Benefits Act 1947.

The biggest entry of the federal government into the health sphere, however, was Medibank. It was created as a public health insurance scheme in recognition of the fact that the private system had proved inadequate in ensuring all Australians had access to healthcare and that extending primary healthcare access to all Australians was cheaper overall than the existing alternative, which could be summed up as 'let people with easily treatable illnesses do nothing until they're so acutely ill that they turn up in hospital emergency wards requiring far more expensive treatments'. The legislation was passed by the Whitlam government in 1974 and began operation on 1 July 1975. The money came from the federal government and was doled out to the states via Healthcare Agreements.

The concept was never popular with the Coalition. Medibank had only been in operation for a few months before the new Fraser government decided that, having spent the previous year blocking legislation establishing a levy to pay for the scheme, it would now introduce a levy to pay for the scheme. It also subsequently removed bulk billing for those not holding a health card, introduced a tax rebate for those with private health insurance, and means-tested access to the system, reconfiguring it from 'universal healthcare' to 'healthcare for those deemed to be at social disadvantage', which was a rather different idea.

Medibank became Medicare in 1984 under the government of Bob Hawke, who returned the system to its previous universal model, and that's more or less how it has remained ever since—although the following years saw increases to the Medicare levy, tax incentives for people to change to private health insurance and alterations to the Healthcare Agreements to shift some of the cost burdens from the federal government to the states.

Hawke might have returned to Whitlam's vision, but he was also the first prime minister to fall afoul of the notion of a co-pay. In 1991, concerned about the rising cost of healthcare, Hawke settled on the idea of instituting a 'co-payment' fee of $3.50 for every GP consultation. This, it transpired, did a lot to poison the party and the broader electorate against his leadership; while it did pass parliament, it was to last a mere three months. That's because, with an election on the horizon and the co-payment being seen as a betrayal of the nation's working classes, it provided a very handy justification for Hawke's treasurer, Paul Keating, to make his successful leadership challenge. The Keating government gleefully eliminated the co-pay in March 1992.

With that sobering lesson in place, it would be a very confident or a very foolhardy government that would dare raise the spectre of a GP co-pay again.

———

The first whispers of a co-payment, initially rumoured to be $6 per visit, had surfaced as soon as the Abbott government took power and was angrily dismissed as a Labor smear by the new foreign minister and deputy leader, Julie Bishop, in January 2014.[2]

She must therefore have been terribly, *terribly* embarrassed when Dutton confirmed a few days later that, sure, it was on the table as part of his planned overhaul of Medicare being undertaken by the Commission of Audit.

'One important job of the Abbott government is to grow the opportunity for those Australians who can afford to do so to contribute to their own healthcare costs,' he explained to the ABC in February. 'If they have a means to contribute to their own healthcare, we should be embarking on a discussion about how that payment model will work.'

And embarking on such an opportunity-growing discussion sounded perfectly reasonable, assuming that one ignored the existing tax rebates for private medical insurance and the commensurate penalties Australians faced for not having it, which presumably would be right in the sweet spot of

---

2 What Bishop actually said was: 'I'm in the Cabinet. This has never been proposed. This is not before the Cabinet . . . We have no plan for a co-payment.' So technically she didn't deny it could yet become policy, if you feel inclined to play semantics.

appealing to those Australians with the means to contribute to their own healthcare. And that was just the first of the difficulties in selling a co-payment as being some sort of reasonable user-pays system.

Another was the more class-warfare-ish element. Sure, as Dutton pointed out, this amount was really only what two of your fancy inner-city lattes cost—how could anyone possibly complain about such a meagre sum? Sadly for the minister, it was immediately clear who this change would affect most. And it wasn't hipsters.[3]

The sort of people who would be affected most were the elderly, especially those with chronic health issues. Children, too, would be affected—especially young ones, who need multiple doctor visits early in life—and people with disabilities or conditions that required regular monitoring. A co-payment would also disproportionately affect the working poor, who were not only more likely to have health issues but also most likely to have the type of job that requires a doctor's note in order to take sick leave. In other words, those towards the bottom of the socio-economic pile would be the ones forced to stump up money for consultations they couldn't avoid.

However, even that might have been imbued with a sense of making sacrifices for the greater good had the government argued that this co-payment money would be going into the health budget, in order to keep the system funded. But it was made clear from the outset that this wasn't the plan at all.

---

3   In the interests of full hipster disclosure, the majority of this book was written on a Macbook in cafés in Sydney's inner west (mainly Natty's in Stanmore) by a bearded man with black-rimmed glasses, often while wearing a checked shirt. My bike, however, has gears.

No, the idea was that this would send a 'price signal'.

Partially designed to prevent 'avoidable GP visits' (presumably based on the assumption that thousands of bored Australians were flagrantly running up national health costs by regularly visiting their GP for kicks), this price signal was also intended to discourage the drain of GPs 'over servicing', which sounded like a somewhat spurious motivation considering the absence of sandwich board wearing doctors standing outside their practices and aggressively soliciting passers-by to pop in for recreational immunisations.

'Putting a price signal in relation to visits to the doctor and ensuring that the Medicare system is sustainable is a key part of that program,' Joe Hockey explained, defending the May budget's plan for a $7 co-payment for all visits to doctors in the face of Labor and the Greens indicating that they would definitely block any such move.

Dutton made clear that $5 from the $7 per visit raised by this new ta . . . sorry, definitely *not* a tax, the public was assured . . . was to fund a Medical Research Future Fund. This money will go to curing cancer, the government declared. What, you don't like the co-pay? So you want people to get cancer, then? Are you some sort of *cancer-lover*?

Oddly, this argument didn't fly quite as majestically as Dutton had clearly assumed it would, not least because the budget also contained swingeing cuts to medical research—including $80 million from cooperative research centres, $75 million from the Australian Research Council and a devastating $111 million from the CSIRO, making the Abbott government's new enthusiasm for medical research seem a wee bit opportunistic.

It was also undercut by the very scientists who were working in the area. While they were certainly not going to say no to a proposed $20 billion research fund, they were nonetheless politely asking questions like 'Um, how will this actually work?' and 'So, who will be administering the fund?' and 'What criteria will be used to determine what does and doesn't get funding?' and 'Do you actually know what you're talking about?'[4]

Despite the level of public distaste for the plan, Hockey slapped on a brave face and made clear that this was definitely not policy made up off the top of his head but a clearly developed plan that the government had talked about plenty of times before—although it was apparently all discussed in a mysterious frequency that no journalists could hear.

'Effectively the savings in health go into the medical research future fund. And given that all that money is not going to be spent, but the return on the investment from the Medical Research Future Fund will gradually increase over time, the overall benefit of our health reforms is a significant saving to the budget,' he explained during a press conference with a roomful of adult journalists, several of whom asked the not-unreasonable question as to why the government hadn't brought up this absolutely-not-just-invented plan before.

---

4 One of the biggest concerns was that the government was obsessed with the sexy, headline-grabbing 'curing' of diseases rather than the less sexy prevention of diseases or research into disease management, both of which would arguably be more practical uses for this money. They also noted that the fund would appear not to cover what's called 'translational' health—taking the results of research and using them to develop things like diagnostic tools. Coming up with a way to cure a disease is not quite as useful if you're not going to spend any money using that knowledge to, y'know, develop tools to cure the disease.

'We have,' Hockey countered, 'but perhaps you didn't hear it.'[5]

Inexplicably, a standing ovation did not follow.

———

While the public and the medical community were definitely not fans of the co-payment plan, the idea also immediately got the states offside, which was a problem. Most had Liberal premiers at the time who were less than delighted about being thrown under the bus by their federal colleagues,[6] correctly surmising that a cut to the federally funded Medicare would be followed by higher costs from people turning up at state-funded hospitals.

By June it was becoming increasingly clear that the plan would not pass parliament in its existing form, and the PM prepared the ground for a retreat by announcing that he would be open to 'a little bit of refinement here and there' on the co-payment.

While Cabinet continued to insist that a price signal was a non-negotiable piece of policy, by August government back-benchers had joined the chorus and were openly decrying the very idea, arguing that they would be pummelled by voters unless pensioners at least were made exempt. Even Howard-era treasurer Peter Costello thought the idea was political suicide, publicly declaring: 'Sooner or later you have to cut losses. The $7 co-payment . . . it's just not going to happen, so

———

5   Seriously, this was his comeback: that he'd said it and yet everyone had mysteriously overlooked it.

6   In South Australia the potential health cost blowout was one of the factors that helped Liberal challenger Steven Marshall fail to unseat Labor premier Jay Weatherill in March. The premier, who had been supposed to be on the way out, instead squeezed through to form a minority government.

let's move on.' And any hopes the government had of getting the plan through the new Senate were quickly hosed down by Clive Palmer. 'We're not going to have a co-payment of even one cent,' said the man who, at the time, controlled the balance of power in the upper house. 'There'll be none—isn't that good?'

A lesser government would have quietly torpedoed the plan there and then, especially given everything else it had going on. But the GP co-pay lived on until December 2014, when it was clear that this could not possibly win the necessary support. Rather than cut his losses and accept this was a battle that couldn't be won, Abbott was determined that 'refinement' was the answer. Thus Dutton came up with a compromise, making it clear that he was all about looking after the little people while not backing down on the terribly important process of charging for GP visits. The new deal? Goodbye compulsory $7 co-pay, hello new 'optional' $5 co-pay.

This was, in the words of the PM, a 'new and improved proposal which indicates that this is a government which is always capable of listening, learning and improving'. The 'optional' bit was somewhat misleading as it wasn't optional for the GPs themselves; they would find their Medicare rebate cut by $5, but would have the 'option' of recouping this loss by charging patients to make up the difference.[7] It also involved changing the definition of 'rebate' under the terms

---

7   Under this new refinement, pensioners, concession card holders and patients under sixteen were exempt from the rebate. http://www.afr.com/news/politics/national/tony-abbott-dumps-7-gp-copayment-for-5-optional-fee-20141209-123hbp

of Medicare, thereby actually instituting a $20 cut to many of the consultations GPs conducted, and also a freeze on all Medicare indexing until July 2018—presumably in recognition of the fact that there was no possibility that any costs for GPs could potentially rise over the following three years.

Despite these far-more-expensive concessions, this didn't prove to be the win that the government expected. The public didn't appreciate the subtle nuances differentiating the previous upfront payment and the new upfront payment, and Australia's medical fraternity were unexpectedly unenthusiastic about being dunned for a total of $25 on most consultations, and then being expected to shake their patients down to recoup a fraction of the difference.

Perhaps sensing that Dutton wasn't bringing the necessary dynamism and public enthusiasm to health reform, that month he became one of the ministers given exciting new opportunities in the Cabinet reshuffle. He became the Minister for Immigration and Border Control, a portfolio better suited to his particular skill set, since the concerns of affected stakeholders were politically easier to ignore.

Even so, he left on a high, with *Australian Doctor* magazine crowning Dutton the nation's Worst Health Minister in the last thirty-five years. Tasmanian GP Dr Donald Rose was effusive in his praise in the accompanying article, declaring that 'Dutton will be remembered as the dullest, least innovative and most gullible for swallowing the reforms from his think tank . . . Although I am glad he has been demoted, it would have been good if he was still around to take responsibility for the current chaos he has caused.'

—

After the Cabinet reshuffle, new health minister Sussan Ley accepted the inevitable and announced on 15 January 2015 that the co-pay had been abandoned as policy, although she was quick to reassure the public that she would still be aggressively seeking new savings in the portfolio. The PM grandly announced in parliament shortly thereafter that the policy was 'dead, buried and cremated'.[8]

However, it wasn't really. Yes, the politically unpalatable co-pay and rebate cuts had been pushed aside, but the Medicare indexing freeze had been retained.

Yet the important thing was that people had now finally shut the hell up, and during a March Cabinet meeting the PM praised Ley for settling the medical community down while not missing the opportunity to give her predecessor a backhander for failing to do his job, reportedly saying, 'This issue [the co-pay] has been mishandled, it has been mishandled until now.'

Ley's success continued in May with the introduction of changes to the PBS, with the 2015 budget signalling savings the government estimated at $5 billion over five years—by demanding further discounts from pharmaceutical companies for generic and off-patent drugs, by forcing pharmacies to drops prices, and by limiting the eligibility for concession cards that allow patients to receive free medication.

---

8   It has a certain rhetorical rhythm to it, sure, but calling something 'dead, buried and cremated' suggests that the PM has no idea how the funerary process works in Australia. Surely burying the dead before cremating them is an unnecessarily inefficient system? That said, at least Abbott acknowledged that death should precede either activity, rather than following as an unavoidable consequence.

However, Ley still indicated that she hankered for a way to stop ungrateful people grubbying up Medicare with their selfish illnesses, declaring, 'It's definitely good policy to put the right price signals in health to make sure that people value the service they get from doctors.'

In other words, like a reverse Norwegian Blue parrot, the co-payment may not in fact be deceased. Perhaps it is, in fact, merely resting.

9
NOT YOUR AVERAGE JO(K)E

*In which the captain's trusted supply officer explains that
poor people don't have ships*

One of the most notable achievements of the Abbott government was to transform the public perception of the treasurer,
Joe Hockey, from avuncular bloke with a good head on his
shoulders to tone-deaf bully with a dubious understanding
of economics.

During the election campaign he'd been careful to indicate
that his stewardship of the economy would be characterised
by a steady hand on the economic tiller, with no surprises and
no sudden changes of direction.

Even then, however, this trajectory seemed unlikely. In
2012 he'd delivered a speech entitled 'The End of the Age of
Entitlement' to the Institute of Economic Affairs in London
which neatly outlined what his approach to his new job would
be, heralding an exciting new age of free market economics to
replace the inefficient hand of the nanny state and all that 'social

safety net' nonsense for which people had worked all their lives. He declared such spending 'unsustainable', as opposed to the more accurate 'we'd have to raise taxes, after governments have been merrily cutting them for short-term political ends for the last two decades, and we're choosing not to do that'.

The fact that the election-period Hockey was saying wildly different stuff to the immediately pre- and post-election Hockey wasn't a problem, because he knew that his legacy wasn't going to be tarnished by irrelevant questions like 'Were you lying?' or 'Seriously, have you any idea what you're doing?' Indeed, so certain was he that glory lurked just around the corner, he assented to being the subject of Madonna King's extraordinary hagiography, *Not Your Average Joe*.

This was the sort of book that any sane politician would have quietly discouraged on the grounds that, sure, it's nice to have just become federal treasurer, but there's an outside chance that having a publication celebrating one's unimpeachable legacy is . . . well, a bit hubris-y.

The book painted an unconsciously unflattering portrait of the man holding the nation's purse strings—from an unpopular kid at the expensive private school to which his immigrant parents worked hard to send him to an angry bully in student politics at Sydney University who playfully confessed to ballot stuffing to win pre-selection. While no doubt intended to show that he was a dedicated battler with a whatever-it-takes attitude, the picture that emerged instead looked an awful lot like an unpopular young man burdened by the expectations of his father, who learned early to fight dirty and knew how to carry a grudge.

It also made clear that there were plenty of grudges to go around, including against fellow Cabinet members such as Ian Macdonald and Malcolm Turnbull—not to mention that backstabbing former schoolmate who supposedly assured Joe that he wouldn't challenge for the leadership before launching a sneak campaign and winning, and under whom Hockey would be appointed treasurer.[1]

The book was published in July 2014, two months after the release of the budget. It ends with a reference to Hockey and finance minister Mathias Cormann enjoying a well-earned cigar just before the announcement, and idly speculated as to what the public's reaction to the budget might be.[2]

By the time of publication, that question had already been answered.

———

From the moment the Abbott government took power Hockey knew that he was facing a challenging gig as treasurer because he had to pivot very, very quickly from 'No cuts, steady as she goes, committed to all the same things Labor is offering' to 'Oh, actually it turns out that there was a deficit crisis hiding behind this tree, so we need to slash everything.'

1 Lest it wasn't clear enough that there was something far more primal than the notion of public service unpinning Hockey's ambitions, the book also revealed that he had had designs on the prime ministership since childhood. Specifically, according to his father, Joe was determined to be leader of the country when he was two years old. I've known at least one two-year-old whose future ambition was to be a fire engine, and for the same reason as the future treasurer: neither she nor Joe had the faintest idea what those terms meant. You know, *because they were two years old*.
2 In a review of the book I wrote for the late *King's Tribune* newsletter, I likened it to concluding a biography of Austria in 1914, mentioning that Archduke Franz Ferdinand had just been murdered in Sarajevo and wondering if there would be any official response. It was a solid joke, and there was no way I wasn't going to reuse it here.

That was always going to be a difficult sell, especially when it involved doing things like handing over $8.8 billion to the Reserve Bank's Reserve Fund—something which the bank's governor, Glenn Stevens, was okay with, but even he admitted that the bank didn't especially need it and hadn't actually asked for it. Indeed, when the top-up was first mooted, the amount was $6 billion, possibly over several years, rather than nearly $9 billion in a lump during a purported crisis. It looked awfully like the treasurer was deliberately attempting to make the deficit look worse in order to justify the punitive cuts he was about to make.

Still, the beauty of economics is that it's expressed in confusing, opaque terms that make most people's brains crave literally anything else, which meant that as long as Joe spoke nonsense with authority he would largely avoid criticism. The issue, therefore, was keeping that same advantage at those times when he was forced to use human language. And that was going to be a big problem.

Before its release, Hockey had been making clear that his first budget would be all about getting the country back into surplus—a fanciful claim, given his strategies to date, but also one that kept to the easy-to-sell narrative of 'surpluses equal good, deficits equal bad', which had been the mantra of all governments since the Howard era, when treasurer Peter Costello lucked into the job during the mining boom. The minerals windfall had gifted the Howard government a surplus that was clearly a reflection of its spectacular economic management and definitely not a result of pure luck in being a country with a lot of iron ore at a time when China wanted to buy loads of the stuff. And the Howard government had used this once-in-a-lifetime economic gift to create the infrastructure of a modern Australia equipped to face the challenges of a wor . . . actually, nah, it was mainly used on tax cuts for the wealthy.

This was in keeping with a very specific strategy adopted by neo-conservative governments the world over——in the US it's called 'starving the beast'—designed with the intention of ensuring that the rich get a sweet deal at the expense of the government regardless of the economic situation.

It works like this: if the economy is going well, then taxes for the wealthy should be cut, because clearly the government has no good reason to take their money; if the economy is going badly, then taxes for the wealth must be cut, because they are 'job creators' who 'stimulate the economy'.[3] This Howard-era beast-starving meant that Australia didn't have what would have been a very handy cash buffer when the Global Financial Crisis hit, but fortunately that happened under Labor's watch and was therefore proof of its terrible economic management.

This stereotype was handily confirmed in 2012 when Wayne Swan succumbed to political pressure and announced that he'd be pursuing a budget surplus for the Gillard government, ignoring the inconvenient facts that a) this was playing into the Coalition narrative rather than making a clear case for the government on its own terms, b) achieving a surplus

---

3   This isn't limited to governments; it's pretty much standard for the likes of banks and telcos to announce record profits along with thousands of job cuts, or mounting losses necessitating thousands of job cuts. The lesson here is that you really should have just gone ahead with that start-up you dreamed about in high school.

would be a hollow, symbolic victory without any actual particular economic benefit, especially given the amount of suffering required to achieve it, and c) that it would be genuinely impossible without Swan carrying out a series of successful *Ocean's 11*-style casino heists.[4]

Having seen how successful yelling 'surplus!' had been in Opposition, Hockey was quick to adopt it as the be-all and end-all of his first budget.

Things got off to a less-than-stellar start when he and finance minister Mathias Cormann were photographed enjoying their aforementioned cigar summit outside the Treasury on Friday, 9 May, having just signed off on the budget.[5] Given that the document had been flagged as downright austere, with brutal cuts that were correctly assumed to affect those at the bottom very harshly, there was a feeling abroad that perhaps the nation's economic stewards should be a little more wary of looking like heartless plutocrats in a Depression-era editorial cartoon. In Joe's defence, he maintained that same tone-deafness right through the budget announcement, in which he declared that Australia is 'a nation of lifters, not leaners' and that 'the age of entitlement is over'.

Of course, as sometimes happens, some entitlements were less over than others.

In the not-so-over basket were things like tax-minimisation schemes for the wealthy (particularly the tax benefits for

---

4   Don't even pretend you're not visualising a catsuit-clad Wayne Swan rappelling down the side of the Crown Melbourne right this minute.
5   There was a predictable flurry of outrage as the photo was shared on Twitter, but the winner was probably author Jane Caro's 'There's nothing like the satisfying flavour of other people's hopes & dreams going up in smoke'.

superannuation). The mining industry was also entitled to exciting new tax breaks for non-profitable operations, a range of new subsidies (including exemption from fuel excise rises) and a $3.4 billion tax break with the abolition of the Minerals Resource Rent Tax (aka the mining tax). There were also plans for major infrastructure projects—specifically roads (and specifically not public transport projects).

In the definitely over basket, however, were such unnecessary things as regulated tertiary education fees and universal healthcare, which included the $7 co-payment for all doctor visits.

That basket also contained public broadcasting, as the ABC and SBS faced immediate cuts—including the complete abolition of the Australia Network, which the ABC had been contracted to create for broadcast to the world, particularly China, the Middle East and the Asia-Pacific region.[6]

Those greedy unemployed and disabled people faced lower benefits, tighter eligibility criteria and, in the case of jobless people under thirty, a six-month wait for unemployment benefits (which would only be available for six months at a time, thereby reflecting the diurnal cycle of Australian young people who apparently hibernate for half a year and therefore don't need food or shelter), along with the return of the Work for the Dole program that had proved expensive and ineffective under the Howard government. 'Young people should be earning or learning,' Rhymin' Joe intoned during his budget

---

6   Oddly enough, the gap left by the death of the Australia Network was filled by Sky News—the broadcasting network part owned by that nice Rupert Murdoch fellow who was such a fine friend of Tony Abbott's. What a lovely and entirely serendipitous outcome!

speech, finally putting the blame for youth unemployment squarely where it belonged: on the shoulders of the young unemployed, who were clearly just lazing around rather than running mining companies or forming lucrative international resource conglomerates.

Those who thoughtlessly failed to die before retirement would also be penalised: there would be pension indexing, cuts to senior concessions, the elimination of the Seniors supplement and a rise in pension age to seventy. Families with kids were also to be taught a valuable lesson, with family tax benefits slashed; those payments that were not limited or eliminated were frozen, regardless of inflation.

And despite Tony Abbott's insistence that he was to be the Indigenous PM, there was the curious decision to slash 150 programs and half a billion dollars in funding for such fripperies as Aboriginal health services and legal aid.

Don't think that Hockey expected the wealthy to get off entirely, though. There was also the inclusion of a new 2 per cent 'debt levy' (which was a *levy*, see, and therefore totally not a new tax) with a threshold set to begin at $180,000. And importantly, unlike the aforementioned cuts, said tax was only going to apply for three years.

'We will all share in more jobs, greater wealth and greater prosperity,' Hockey insisted as he delivered the budget in parliament, before accepting the government's applause and taking his seat, confident that he'd cemented his legacy.

———

Weirdly enough, the budget didn't go down quite as well with people outside the Coalition.

Sure, the other major parties were predictably scathing. Bill Shorten dismissed it as 'the conscious development of an underclass' and disputed the economic modelling, declaring it 'a budget that will push up the cost of living for every Australian family . . . drawn up by people who have never lived from pay cheque to pay cheque', while Greens leader Christine Milne was similarly livid: 'I have never witnessed such a brazen attempt by any prime minister to ruthlessly and so quickly impose such a vindictive, hard-right, cruel and ideological agenda on the Australian people and our environment and then try to justify it by deliberately concocting a fake national budget emergency.'

Experts were not much more complimentary. Frank Jotzo, director of the Centre for Climate Economics and Policy at the Australian National University, pointed out that the mining and carbon tax repeals would take billions from government revenue, aside from their environmental effects: ' . . . the proposed changes to climate policy will be a cost to the budget bottom line of around $16 billion over the next four years, and a total of probably over $20 billion between now and 2020. At the same time, much less will be achieved with far lower carbon emission reductions.'

The Australian Council of Social Service didn't mince words in its analysis document, entitled 'A Budget that Divides the Nation'. In her introduction ACOSS CEO Professor Cassandra Goldie declared: 'Rather than bringing us together in a truly fair, shared effort, this budget entrenches divisions in our community: between young and old and people on high incomes and those struggling to make ends meet. It threatens to destroy the social safety net that has served our nation well . . . the budget will damage far more than it repairs.'

But again, these were just eggheads and socialists, right? The government had already made clear how little their opinion was going to count for anything in the exciting new Abbott-scape. What possibly came as more of a surprise, however, was the reaction from the likes of News Corp, who could generally be relied on to lead the cheers for the government. The tone could be surmised from the title of a news.com article entitled 'Australians think Federal Budget 2014 is the worst in a very, very long time'. It began: 'It's a total stinker and it's been a long time since we've seen anything like it,' before castigating the government for a number of broken election promises, including the GP co-payment, and concluding: 'It's clear Mr Abbott has fallen flat on his face. The big question is whether he'll be able to get back up again.'

Opinion polls showed universal scorn for the budget, with a staggering 75 per cent of respondents to the post-budget Galaxy poll declaring they'd be left worse off. Even those who cautiously supported the general thrust of the budget towards smaller government and deficit reduction warned that savage cuts would not do the trick. They especially factored in the cost of redundancies and the effect that slashing industry subsidies (including to the automotive industry, essentially ending any chance of it remaining in Australia) and the loss of 16,000 public sector jobs would have on the unemployment rate.

Hockey, however, was bullish, declaring that the first Howard budget had been equally unpopular and yet that government had powered through successfully. The problem with his optimistic version of history was that it was demonstrably wrong: Costello's first budget had been actually pretty well received, and the Howard government's approval rating had gone up three points rather than, as happened with Hockey, dropping to eleven points behind Labor, with the leader's approval rating slumping to minus 30 per cent.

This was the first moment when it dawned on the party that maybe Joe Hockey was something of a liability.

———

As the chorus of disapproval rose in volume, the government held fast to its determination that the budget would pass parliament—despite it becoming apparent that most of the measures outlined therein would be defeated in the Senate. Clive Palmer declared that his PUP bloc would reject the health, welfare and education cuts, the GP co-payment and the 'debt levy' temporary tax increase on the wealthy. He also called out the idea that Australia was in a debt crisis, calling it 'more bullshit being fed to the Australian public for the Abbott government's consumption'. The government was able to trumpet the successful passage of its mining and carbon tax repeals, but it was now stymied on its other signature measures.

However, despite all the kerfuffle following the budget, it was discussion of the fuel excise that gave Hockey the opportunity to lay bare his understanding of how Australia's battling classes were faring.

A push to increase the taxation on fuel had been rejected by Labor in the Senate, but the government had, not unreasonably, expected the Greens to support the move. After all, it was in keeping with their environmental philosophy: more expensive petrol would encourage less driving and, therefore, less burning of high-carbon fossil fuels. Instead, the Greens opposed the proposal, arguing that, since the revenue would go towards building new roads, this would ultimately increase the amount of pollution rather than discourage motorists.

It was a gift to the government—a perfect opportunity to argue that the Greens were environmental hypocrites who selected their principles as it suited them. And thus in August, on ABC radio in Brisbane,[7] Hockey rose to the occasion.

'Now, I'll give you one example,' he offered. 'The change to fuel excise, the people that actually pay the most are higher-income people, with an increase in fuel excise, and yet, the Labor Party and the Greens are opposing it.

'They say you've got to have wealthier people or middle-income people pay more. Well, change to the fuel excise does exactly that. The poorest people either don't have cars or actually don't drive very far in many cases. But they are opposing what is meant to be, according to the Treasury, a progressive tax.'

And all hell broke loose.

———

The issue with Hockey's statement about poor people wasn't just that it was nonsense, but that it was the sort of nonsense that people could immediately recognise.

For a start, the idea that poor people didn't drive in Australia was easy to reject outright. Simple demographics made the reality clear: most jobs in Australian cities cluster around

---

7   The entire transcript still exists on the Treasury website, because why wouldn't Hockey want to celebrate his victory? http://jbh.ministers.treasury.gov.au/transcript/075-2014/

the CBD and inner suburbs, the exact areas where poor people couldn't afford to live. Lower-income people have historically lived in the outer western suburbs of the state capitals (except in Adelaide and Perth, where the outer west would be in the ocean). Due to Australia's less-than-stellar public transport system, especially in outer suburbs, and the realities of low-income and especially casual work where excuses like 'there was trackwork on the western line' are more likely to be received with termination than sympathy, people on low incomes are far more likely to accept the expense of running a car than have their employment depend on unreliable trains and often-absent buses.

Hockey's tone-deaf response seemed to confirm every stereotype about the government generally and the Coalition specifically: that they had no idea about the realities of life for the majority of working Australians.

It also ignored the reality of all flat taxes: they affect the poor more than the wealthy because, while they both pay the same amount, that amount is a bigger proportion of the income of someone without much money than someone with plenty of the stuff. An extra cost of $10 a week makes little difference to someone clearing $5000 a month after expenses, but is crippling for someone ending each week with $15 left in their pocket.

The negative impression of Hockey's compassion wasn't alleviated by Joe angrily sticking to his guns.[8] He was 'just pointing out the facts', as he insisted on Sydney radio station

8   ABC's FactCheck has a great analysis of the ABS data and the Treasury's interpretation thereof. http://www.abc.net.au/news/2014-08-15/joe-hockey-poor-people-cars-claim-misleading/5671168

2UE. 'The fact of the matter is that I can only get the facts out there and explain the facts, how people interpret them is up to them,' he said, adding that the Australian Bureau of Statistics backed him up.

The odd thing about Joe's spirited defence of the ABS data was that the Treasury's calculations dramatically underestimated the effect of increased fuel prices on various households, compared to the ABS's own analysis. It transpired that this was based on a difference of 'assumptions' in the data—specifically, that the government chose to interpret non-responses to the census as low-income households without cars rather than as unoccupied housing (holiday houses, abandoned buildings, that sort of thing), which is what the ABS did. Once the extra 1.5 million non-response households were taken out of the data set, the cost of an increase in fuel to low-income households shot up dramatically. So this could be interpreted as 'difference in assumptions', sure. Or it could be interpreted as 'a very deliberate effort to manipulate the data to achieve a desired outcome'.

As the public debate raged, Hockey finally caved in and after two days apologised, complaining that people were just being mean. He was, he assured 2GB listeners, 'really, genuinely sorry that there is any suggestion, any suggestion at all that I or the government does not care for the most disadvantaged in the community. I am sorry about that interpretation, I am sorry about the words . . . As everyone who knows me knows, all of my life I have fought for and tried to help the most disadvantaged in the community, and for there to be some suggestion that I had evil in my heart when it comes to the most disadvantaged is upsetting, but it is more upsetting for those people, so I want to make it perfectly clear to the community if there is any suggestion that I had evil in my heart or that I don't care about you then I am sorry about that.'

You might notice that this apology was largely about how people clearly misinterpreted his intentions, as opposed to him being in some way mistaken or incorrect. There was no acceptance that the problem was what he said rather than the unkind manner in which it had been interpreted. In this, he was keeping to script with a standard government non-apology, because admitting fault is what lesser people do.[9] But at least he'd learned his lesson and would never, ever make another stupid statement in public again.

Probably.

---

9   A note on non-apologies: these are things that sound like apologies while not admitting fault and, in fact, subtly accusing the victim of being in the wrong. Typically they take the form of 'I'm sorry if anyone was offended', which makes clear that the speaker's only crime was being too gosh-darn honest to a bunch of overly sensitive crybabies. It's an instructive insight into a person's character, since too few people wear t-shirts helpfully explaining 'I am a vengeful narcissist'.

10
MEET THE NEW SENATE!

*In which we meet the freebooting mavericks of
the crossbench*

This seems as good a time as any to have a look at what happened in the rough-and-tumble upper house after the 2013 election.

While the Abbott government loudly and repeatedly cried that the Australian people had given it a 'mandate!' to enact policies that it had failed to actually mention ahead of the election, there was a teensy-tiny problem. Or, more specifically, eight of them.

The Abbott government had indeed achieved a landslide victory in the House of Representatives, but the nation's apparent hunger for change had failed when it came to the Senate. Inexplicably, the people of Australia didn't hand the Coalition the majority in the Senate to which it naturally felt entitled.

At this election forty of the seventy-six Senate seats were contested[1] and three of the future crossbench were not up for election and were thus known quantities.

For a start, the government knew that two South Australian senators were staying put: Bob Day of the ultra-conservative Christian party Family First, from whom the government correctly assumed it could generally expect support, and the popular, outspoken, vaguely left-leaning independent Nick Xenophon, who originally was elected on a platform of gambling reform and who—again correctly—the government assumed would be a problem.[2] The other incumbent was another religious conservative: Victorian Democratic Labour Party senator John Madigan, who was still a wee bit too leftie for the government's comfort.

As the votes were tallied and the labyrinthine web of preferences shook out, it became apparent that a surprising number of votes had been cast for micro parties and that the post-July 2014 Senate would probably have a larger than usual number of independents in it. The question was who, specifically, they would end up being.

While Labor languished and the Greens' primary vote decreased, the surprise success was the Palmer United Party. It had spent a vast amount of Clive Palmer's money aggressively

---

1   Quick parliamentary note: MPs serve three-year terms, as do the two senators each from the ACT and the NT, while senators from the other states enjoy a more luxurious six.

2   In fact, when the *Sydney Morning Herald* crunched the numbers in May 2015 ('The surprise findings of who's backing who', 21 May 2015), it found that Day had voted with the government for 90 per cent of the divisions, making him the most supportive member of the crossbench. Xenophon, meanwhile, was the least on board with only 30 per cent, below even that of Labor (but well above the Greens).

advertising itself as the outsider voice of working Australia with the sorts of grassroots credentials that only a billionaire mining baron could boast. The party enjoyed initial success in Queensland with the election of former sports star Glenn Lazarus and in Tasmania with the little-known Jacqui Lambie.[3]

The Liberal Democrats also enjoyed a jump in support, which they put down to Australia embracing its strongly free-market libertarian views and everyone else put down to having been first on the ballot paper in NSW and having the word 'Liberal' in its name, thereby confusing hasty voters. That was certainly the position that the Coalition took, regarding David Leyonhjelm as having stolen a NSW Senate seat that was rightfully its and making empty legal threats about forcing the party to change its name.

However, the biggest surprise came from the Australian Motoring Enthusiast Party, a political offshoot of founder Keith Littler's day job as creator of the Grunt Files series of custom car videos.

Thanks to the work of 'preference whisperer' Glenn Druery, the AMEP's Victorian candidate and unemployed timber worker Ricky Muir was elected to the Senate despite winning 0.51 per cent of the vote, which grew to 14.3 per cent after preferences. Astonishingly, Muir had only been made the party's candidate four months before the election without actually having met anyone from the Queensland-based federal party.

---

3   It's estimated that PUP spent around half a million dollars on their federal campaign, and even that was dwarfed by the million-plus sunk into their failed Tasmanian state election campaign.

So important were the preferences of micro parties that the rest of the Senate makeup was complicated by a hiccup in Western Australia where the Australian Electoral Commission discovered it had misplaced 1375 ballots. Under normal circumstances this would probably have had little effect, but in 2013 it determined two Senate seats. If those ballots weren't included, the winners were Labor's Louise Pratt and PUP's Zhenya 'Dio' Wang. With the votes included, the winners were Greens senator Scott Ludlum and another micro party candidate, the Australian Sports Party's Wayne Dropulich.

There was an immediate and predictable challenge from Labor and PUP in the High Court's Court of Disputed Returns, and after a lot of head shaking the AEC accepted the inevitable and Western Australians returned to the polls on 5 April 2014 to give it another, more careful go. This time the result was definitive: WA's Senate representatives would be three Liberals, one Labor, Ludlum and Wang.

Wang was the most mysterious of the PUP senators. A civil engineer by training, he was CEO of the Palmer-owned Australasian Resources when tapped to run for the party. Even during the campaign he barely ever appeared in public, much less spoke—the two qualities that were also to characterise his subsequent parliamentary career.

And thus was the new Senate makeup determined: of the seventy-six senators, the Coalition had thirty-three, Labor twenty-five, the Greens ten, Palmer United three, and the remaining five were independents and micro parties.

It was a great result for Palmer, made even greater since Muir had confirmed in October 2013 that he would form a voting bloc with PUP. With Palmer's control of four of the eight crossbench votes, the government would require his support for any legislation to pass—assuming, as it largely could, that Madigan and Day would vote along Coalition lines. Palmer's power as kingmaker was all but ensured.

At least, that's how it looked. But by the time the new Senate took its place in parliament, on 1 July 2014, Muir had already distanced himself from PUP, and by November he was voting against the party on proposed changes to financial planning laws. However, by that stage Muir would be the least of the party's problems.

——

The success of micro parties via preference-swapping arrangements gave the larger parties a clear agenda before the next election: ensuring that the ballot paper was changed so that this never happened again.

The Senate ballot paper offered just two options: vote for a single party above the line, or number everything below. And with a record number of candidates running, and the tantalising scent of the traditional Australian voting booth sausage sizzle wafting on the breeze, most voters couldn't be bothered spending fifteen minutes laboriously numbering every individual candidate—not when the alternative was popping a 1 in a box and getting some democracy-meat in their citizen-mouth.

Preferences are determined via negotiations between the various parties in an election and are subsequently registered with the AEC to determine what votes go where. Eventually this almost always trickles down to a vote for one of the major parties, but occasionally it throws up a fortunate independent.

Thus while a 1 for the Coalition, Labor or Greens was probably going to go directly to the party, a 1 for the minor parties was going to bounce like a pachinko ball until finally settling in its eventual home. This meant that a vote for Socialist Alliance might first bounce toward a libertarian-style party like the Australian Sex Party, then might briefly ricochet towards the hard-right Shooters and Fishers before landing, inexplicably, in the basket of votes for the Motoring Enthusiasts.

Given the tiny primary vote that several of the crossbench achieved, it's impossible to argue that the presence of Muir in the Senate represented the direct wishes of the electorate so much as the random interplay of protest votes. And while there's an argument that this actually ensured that someone other than professional career politicians ended up in parliament, it seemed at odds with the notion of direct democracy.

Thus a parliamentary inquiry was immediately convened to examine what might be done to make the Senate vote more directly representational of voter desires, and also conveniently weaken the influence of preference deals. The result of this inquiry was handed down in May 2014 and recommended a system based largely on the NSW upper house ballot, where the voting paper allows above-the-line preferences. Under this system the parties can still cut their deals and recommend their preferences, but the individual voter can determine in which direction their specific preferences flow. For example, instead of voting for the Socialist Alliance and discovering later that you've actually ended up voting for the Motoring

Enthusiasts, you could choose to direct your preferences as you saw fit.

The Coalition was very much in favour of making these sorts of changes, which was hardly a surprise since most of the micro parties leaned to the right in varying degrees and therefore it hoped reform would funnel more preferences in its direction. Labor could also see obvious advantages to the plan—mainly in the hope of snaring an even greater share of the Greens' preferences. The Greens were in a tougher position because their platform made clear that they supported any move towards a more direct form of democracy, and yet such reform might cost them seats.[4] However, fewer independents would also raise a higher probability of the party holding the sole balance of power in the Senate.

It would definitely not affect the more popular independents—Xenophon would be safe, certainly—but the result for the rest of the crossbench was less reassuring. Certainly any legislation that the government might want to run through parliament could not rely on navigating the crossbench—but it would almost certainly win the support of Labor, the Greens or both.

There was no hurry, of course—after all, the new Senate hadn't even sat at this point. But this was a change the government could confidently trust would get over the line, should it become expedient to call a double dissolution—not least since

---

4 That being said, the Greens had been slammed by preference deals in the 2013 election: leaving aside the anti-Greens strategies of Labor and the Coalition, WikiLeaks' failure to support the Greens in WA almost ended Scott Ludlam's career, and Nick Xenophon's decision to put the majors ahead of the party in SA almost cost Sarah Hanson-Young hers.

Abbott had signalled unambiguously that he had no interest in negotiating with the crossbench, whoever they were.

———

The history of minor parties in Australia is not a litany of triumphs. Small parties have a tendency to turn up, make a lot of noise and then implode messily, especially if they're based around one charismatic—or at least notorious—leader. Julian Assange's much-hyped WikiLeaks Party didn't even get to the point of enjoying the brief heyday of Pauline Hanson's One Nation before things fell into the inevitable slew of accusations and lawsuits, falling to bits ahead of winning an insignificant amount of the vote.[5]

Of the other minor parties hoping to make their debut on the federal stage, the Sex Party publicly savaged Liberal Democrat David Leyonhjelm as having deliberately scuttled its chances by not honouring their preference deal and failing to submit his preferences to the AEC. For his part, Leyonhjelm blamed the complexities of today's complicated fax technology for an innocent error.

The Sports Party's brief moment of hope was extinguished in the WA re-election, and the Victorian office of the Motoring Enthusiast Party had disintegrated under furious battles over whether or not its Facebook page had been officially vetted by the federal party in October 2013, long before Ricky Muir even stepped into the chamber for the first time.

---

5 Specifically, 0.66 per cent. There was no small amount of controversy about the party, not least when it was revealed that it was preferencing some questionable groups ahead of the Greens, with whom it shared most of its principles, and the fallout saw high-profile Victorian candidate Leslie Cannold leave the party. Of course, the party wasn't helped by the fact that its leader, Julian Assange, was still holed up in the Ecuadorian embassy in London to avoid facing sexual assault charges in Sweden for fear of being extradited to the US.

The spirit in the larger minor parties was not exactly ebullient either.

The Nationals had long since ceased to exist independently of the Liberal Party in any meaningful way (indeed, in Queensland and the Northern Territory they've long been the same thing), but the Victorian and NSW elections demonstrated that its biggest threat was not the growing chasm between the Coalition partners on the increasingly fraught relationship between miners and pastoralists: changing demographics and the destruction of farmland for mining interests was fast eroding the regional vote in favour of the Greens.

And while the Greens were in the ascendant, any time they might feel as though they were making progress towards being a powerful third force in Australia, they presumably felt an icy breath on their necks from the ghost of the Australian Democrats—a party that was once seen as the sensible centre in national politics, even holding the balance of power in the heady days of 1998. However, the Democrats' fractious 1999 deal to support the Howard government's GST demolished public trust in the party and the party's own internal concord, and by April 2015 it was arguing with the Australian Electoral Commission about whether or not the party even existed.[6]

And into this charred and barren landscape strode a bold

---

6   There had been two factions among the seven-strong Democrat Senate team in 1999: the majority led by party leader Meg Lees, and two dissenters. One dissenter was Natasha Stott-Despoja, who went on to replace Lees in a bitter leadership battle; the other was Andrew Bartlett, who went on to replace Stott-Despoja and has since joined the Greens. The last sitting Democrat was defeated in 2009, and in April 2015 the party was officially deregistered as a political party by the Australian Electoral Commission. At the time of writing it was planning to challenge the AEC's decision, although it's not really clear why it would bother.

new player: Palmer United.

———

If you're reading this from the future you might be thinking, 'Wow, that Palmer United Party really got itself in a sweet, sweet position, where it was effectively the gatekeeper of legislation in the Senate—why, to use the parlance of the time, that sounds as though it would have been very "disruptive"!'

First up, future person, please don't ever say 'disruptive'. That's an odious term that the hucksters of 2015 used when they wanted to extort money from wealthy business folks terrified that they were no longer 'with it'. It's like 'synergy' or 'proactive': a term that exists purely as a challenge to the listener. 'Go on,' it seems to say, 'I fucking dare you to call me out on my bullshit. You won't though, will you? No, you'll smile, you'll nod, and you'll employ me as your social media strategist.'[7]

Also, at the risk of giving away later plot twists, PUP wasn't nearly the game-changer that everyone hoped-slash-feared. Palmer turned out to be kinda like Rutger Hauer in *Blade Runner*: at first he appeared huge, deadly-looking and unnaturally blond, before collapsing all-but-alone having done much less than anyone would have reasonably expected. Sad though it may seem for the party that promised to shake up the staid two-party system, the golden age of PUP was mainly restricted to the period before the new Senate was sworn in.

The fact that Palmer won his Queensland reps seat of

———

[7] Yes, that was also a thing in our time. For some reason companies genuinely thought that they'd lose market share if their products weren't individually harassing you on Facebook. For example, for several months a former *Time Out* colleague was paid not-inconsiderable amounts of human dollars to pretend to be a popular cowboy-themed ice cream on Twitter. In many ways it was a more innocent world.

Fairfax by a whopping thirty-six votes should have been an early indication that perhaps he didn't command quite the popular groundswell of support that he seemed to assume. However, the period immediately after the election was the point at which the possibilities of the three-and-a-Muir Senate bloc seemed endless and magical, with Clive in the lower house explaining exactly how his minions were going to change things as soon as the Senate sat.[8]

Importantly, the party's success wasn't limited to just federal politics either: in the Queensland parliament, there were two former LNP-turned-independent-turned-PUP MPs, Alex Douglas and Carl Judge, and in the Northern Territory parliament three disgruntled former Country Liberal Party members of the Legislative Assembly jumped ship to join PUP in April 2014: Alison Anderson, Larisa Lee and Francis Xavier Kurrupuwu. While the party failed to secure any electoral gains in the South Australian or Tasmanian state elections in March 2014, it still looked look like there could be a proper movement happening in the Top End.

Unfortunately, despite this auspicious beginning, the party started to splinter almost immediately.

There is a lot of speculation as to why exactly people seemed so determined to put the lie to the party's name, but the short answer appeared to be that the 'Palmer' bit was in

---

8   It's worth pointing out that 'Clive in the lower house' is a little misleading: the main thing that the Member for Fairfax became known for was not actually turning up. In 2014 he was the MP most absent, managing to make it for a mere forty-nine of the seventy-six sitting days. Some of that was because of the birth of his second child, to be fair, but the rest he put down to political tactics such as not wanting to indicate how the party would vote in the Senate. Or maybe just wanting to have a lie in.

direct conflict with the 'United' bit.

As mentioned previously, Palmer wasn't just a billionaire mining magnate with a sideline in golf courses, animatronic dinosaurs and building replicas of doomed passenger liners: he was also a disgruntled former LNP supporter who felt his political ambitions were not being met, and therefore PUP could be seen as an act of very expensive revenge against the party that had spurned him. But while revenge is an excellent motivator, it's not a great long-term strategy for a political party—especially a very new one attempting to stretch its influence over state and federal politics. That would be a challenge for any party machine, even a well-established one.

The party's first month in the Senate was a big one, helping to pass the abolition of the carbon and mining taxes but—surprisingly—blocking the repeal of the Renewable Energy Target and the Clean Energy Fund.

The wheels started to come off shortly thereafter.

First to bail was Queensland's Alex Douglas on 11 August 2014 after a mere two months, declaring that he'd left the LNP because of what he saw as 'cronyism' and that PUP had proved no different—and thus, he would be continuing his political career as an independent.

In the NT, Kurrupuwu was next, jumping ship in September to rejoin the CLP. Carl Judge had actually been made leader of the party in Queensland in March 2014, but even this singular honour wasn't enough to dissuade him from announcing on 8 October 2014 that he was once again an independent. The two remaining NT MPs, Anderson and Lee, reverted back to independence in November (with Anderson rejoining the CLP the following February).

Federally it was no better. Jacqui Lambie had clashed publicly with Palmer over support for financial advice laws and defence pay cuts, with Palmer describing her as 'berserk'. She quit the party on 24 November 2014.

A Roy Morgan poll at the time indicated that PUP support had dwindled to insignificance around the nation, peaking at an anaemic 4 per cent in its Queensland heartland. However, any hopes that its home state might offer a salve for the ailing party were dashed in January 2015 when PUP picked up zero seats in the state election. The party also missed the registration deadlines for the SA and NSW state elections, meaning that it could only run 'endorsed candidates' as independents without using the PUP brand. Unsurprisingly, this failed to secure any seats.

Incredibly, things got even worse from there. On 13 March 2015 Glenn Lazarus announced that he was also quitting the party, citing a culture of 'bullying behaviour' from Palmer which had ended with the leader sacking Glenn's wife Tess Lazarus from the Canberra PUP office. This left Palmer and Wang as the only remaining members of the party in political office at any level, and in May 2015 Palmer announced that PUP would no longer bother to contest state elections. Which seemed shrewd: after all, it was much cheaper to not run campaigns than to run them, especially when the results were identical.

Thus it seemed all over bar the shouting for the party—and maybe the shouting was also over, given that Wang seemed determined to maintain his career-long policy of unbroken public silence.

Would it rise, phoenix-like, from the ashes of their once-fiery aspirations? Time would tell.[9]

---

9   Although the more superstitious-minded might have looked at the mysterious electrical fire that burned down Palmer's beloved animatronic T-Rex Jeff in may 2015 and thought, 'Hmmm, possibly not the best of omens, that.'

11
SOMEONE'S GETTING A SHIRTFRONTIN'

In which the captain contemplates a nice new shirt(front)

In July 2014, something happened on the other side of the world that was to have huge domestic consequences: the seemingly accidental shooting down of Malaysia Airlines flight MH17 over Ukraine in July.

The tragic event drew worldwide attention to the former Soviet republic. Of course, most Australians were vaguely aware that there was something going on over there between Ukraine and Russia, what with Russia annexing the Crimean Peninsula in March and seemingly preparing for a full-scale invasion on Ukraine's northern and eastern borders, but up until this point most of the world seemed okay with leaving them to sort it out between themselves.

Even NATO was reticent to wade in without a formal declaration of war as the Russians whistled nonchalantly, furnished weapons to the separatist militias who sought to align with Russia, and massed its armed forces on the borders in support of conveniently located 'military exercises'. MH17 changed all that, possibly averting (or, at least, postponing) a full-scale invasion in the process.

The flight had left Amsterdam en route to Kuala Lumpur on 17 July when it was struck by a missile and crashed near the Ukraine city of Torez. All 283 passengers and 15 crew were killed.

There was some confusion at first as to exactly what had happened, with the immediate presumption being a terrorist bomb. Before too long, however, the working theory was that the plane had been hit by a surface-to-air missile, presumably after being mistaken for a military aircraft. That the missiles were Russian was based on a few lines of evidence, starting with the fact that Ukraine air force planes had been shot down in June and July, including after the downing of MH17, and continuing with strong evidence of the Russian military supplying local separatist militias with Buk ground-to-air missiles.

There was also the uncomfortable fact that the area from which the missile would have had to be fired was held by separatist troops and that the Ukraine army couldn't have moved missile launchers into that part of the country even if it'd had any to move in the first place, which it appeared it did not.

Moscow strenuously refused to embrace this circumstantial evidence. Conjecturing that the missile had been fired by trigger-happy Ukrainians, it denied any involvement and insisted this was just anti-Russian propaganda and the Ukraine army had probably found some missiles in a ditch or bought them off the internet or something.

While the international attention created by a passenger jet being downed may have contributed to Russia scaling back its invasion plans, this tragedy initially seemed like a possible flashpoint for the conflict to turn into a full-scale war. Indeed, the examination of the crash site—led by Dutch investigators—was at first hampered by the fact that the thirty-five-square-kilometre area over which the debris was strewn was in an active war zone.

There were many (arguably exaggerated) reports of looting and possible tampering with evidence. The majority of the victims of the crash were Dutch, with forty-three from Malaysia and thirty-eight Australians,[1] and, while most of the governments (especially the Netherlands) were determined to have all of the facts before launching into what would definitely be a criminal trial, if not a specific war crime tribunal, Tony Abbott wasn't about to let diplomacy stop him from naming names.

———

There appeared to be little doubt in the minds of most world leaders that this was a horrible accident and that what most likely happened was that Russian-backed separatists had shot down a passenger jet after mistaking it for a military aircraft.

However, international leaders generally had the good sense to let the investigation proceed without giving the

1   There is some disagreement as to the exact number. It appears that there were twenty-seven people travelling on Australian passports, but several of the victims were partners and children of Australian passport-holders, leading to the generally accepted death toll of thirty-eight.

Russian government an excuse to declare the whole thing an insult and flounce off. While the likes of UK prime minister David Cameron and US president Barack Obama expressed their horror and promised justice would be served, they were careful to articulate their support for the investigation and respect for whatever conclusions it eventually drew rather than directly accuse Russia of involvement.[2]

There was another reason why leaders might have felt that it was unwise to rattle their sabres too loudly: the imminent meeting of the Group of Twenty (G20) in Brisbane, which would put all said leaders in the one room—including Russia's colourful president, Vladimir Putin. However, the fact that he was hosting the meeting didn't prevent Abbott from calling a shovel a brutal, cold-blooded murderer.

'This aircraft didn't come down through accident. It was shot down. It did not crash, it was downed and it was downed over territory controlled by Russian-backed rebels,' he declared to the media in July. 'It was downed by a missile which seems to have been launched by Russian-backed rebels . . . This really is a test for Russia. It really is a test for Russia—how transparent and fair dinkum is it going to be? There can be no excuses. No buck-passing. No blame-shifting. There has to be absolute full cooperation with an impartial international inquiry.'

The suggestion that Russian's dinkum was insufficiently fair didn't go down at all well in Moscow: 'Without bothering

---

2   The report is scheduled to be handed down in October 2015, so by the time you read this you'll already know the result. Actually, we all probably know the result already—but you'll have a better idea of the degree of angry accusations from Russia that the whole thing's a NATO plot secretly backed by the Americans.

himself about evidence and operating only on speculation, Mr T. Abbott assigned guilt,' said a Russian foreign ministry spokesperson, who wasn't about to use the PM's entire first name.[3] 'Abbott's statements are unacceptable.'

Unacceptable to Russian audiences, maybe, but at home the PM soon discovered that his tough talk was paying dividends. His domestic approval rating, which had taken a nosedive after the budget, started to show signs of life. Giving Russia what for, and raising the terror threat from medium to high, clearly resonated with a significant propor-tion of the Australian electorate; Abbott's approval rating rose by ten points between mid-July and September to a high of 41 per cent.[4]

And thus on 13 October, confident in the popularity of his take-no-prisoners rhetoric, he delivered a line that was to turn it all around: 'Look, I'm going to shirtfront Mr Putin. You bet you are—you bet I am,' he stumblingly said of the oft-shirtless president. 'I am going to be saying to Mr Putin, "Australians were murdered. They were murdered by Russian-backed rebels using Russian-supplied equipment. We are very unhappy about this." '

———

The choice of words was . . . interesting.

Abbott is a Sydneysider and thus it was possible that he didn't know what it meant to 'shirtfront' someone. In Australian Rules football, shirtfronting is a full-body front-on

---

3   Or perhaps he had legitimately confused our PM with 1980s *A-Team* star and jewellery enthusiast, Mr T?

4   As it happens, that was also the approval rating he boasted at the time of the election.

tackle designed to basically knock the wind out of one's opponent. It's not technically illegal, but it'd get you sent off these days. There's an argument that maybe Abbott thought it referred to one of those alpha-male moves where one yanks a chap in by his shirt, just below the collar, in order to tell them they'd better start toeing the line if they don't want to be choking on their own teeth. It's a marvellously masculine image and would probably have done the PM a load of good—had the world not responded by openly laughing at him.

Said laughter started early and, as befitted a propaganda gift to the Putin administration, was predictably led by the Russian media. *Pravda*'s Timothy Bancroft-Hinchey called it 'the most blatant example of shit-faced ignorance and pig-headed arrogance the world has seen since the likes of Hitler or Pol Pot . . . a disturbed mind crying out for therapy'— a message this commentator maintained through a series of gleeful interviews with the Western press. Anissa Naouai, the English-speaking host on news channel Russia Today, ran footage of Abbott making his threat, intercut with Putin's judo work and the question: 'Tony Abbott, you sure you want to chest-bump Vladimir Putin?'

While Russians leaped to their leader's defence, the same didn't happen in Australia. Jokes regarding shirts—normally accompanied by photos of the Speedo-clad PM—were all the rage, and the meme-savvy corners of the internet were immediately flooded with Putin Shirtfront tees.

And it didn't take long for Abbott to start walking his statement back. By 14 October the language had become:

'Well, we're going to have a very robust conversation, a very, very robust conversation, because plainly thirty-eight innocent Australians were murdered.'

Russia's second secretary at the embassy in Canberra, Alexander Odoevsky, politely listened to such claims and then gently pointed out that Putin's summit calendar was already full and there was no time scheduled for this supposedly robust discussion.

'There has not been a request for a bilateral at the Brisbane summit from either side,' he said, with typically Russian élan. 'So we are not sure when the prime minister would like to shirtfront the Russian president.' He added wryly: 'I know Prime Minister Abbott is a very keen bicyclist. The Russian president does a lot of judo.'

Perhaps worried about getting pinned to the mat, Abbott backed further down as the date grew closer. On 10 November in Beijing he made clear that he 'will just be looking for an assurance from the president that what they said then, they meant, and what they said then is still what they say now'. Which, as statements go, is a good deal less than 'I'm going to shirt front Mr Putin. You bet you are.'

The PM looked even less powerful when his subsequent requests for a meeting with Putin were cheerfully rebuffed by Russian officials ahead of the G20. So the narrative changed again: now, when questioned about his plans for confronting the Russian leader, the PM would angrily respond that it didn't matter and that getting answers from the Russian leader was 'by no means the biggest part of the agenda that Australia is following'.

Abbott *did* finally get his confrontation with Putin at the G20, though. Well, not a confrontation per se, but a robust discussion.

Okay, maybe it wasn't entirely robust, or indeed much of a discussion.

Alright, fine: it was 'a brief and polite chat', according to a spokesperson for the PM, before Putin left the summit early—ostensibly because he was tired.[5]

And thus were the innocent victims of that terrible day avenged: briefly and politely.

———

Abbott was arguably right that, among his nation's priorities at the G20, Shirtfrontgate wasn't that big a deal for Australians—but only because there were other issues in which the public was interested, and which unfortunately reflected even less well on the government.

The main one was, predictably, climate change. It had been a big topic at previous G20s, but had been conspicuously left off the agenda for this one—presumably since all that global warming stuff had been pretty much sorted out.

So the Australian government must have been very surprised when the topic kept coming up, and annoyed by how much attention everyone paid to the historic—and impressively ambitious—emissions trading scheme hashed out between Barack Obama and China's president Xi Jinping even as Abbott emphasised that climate change wasn't really

---

5 Putin chose to fly home, rather than hop a lift with one of the Russian warships that just so happened to putter along Australia's northern maritime border at the time of the conference. Say what you will about the Russian leader, the man has an undeniable flair for the theatrical.

worth talking about and how coal was totally the happenin' fuel of tomorrow.[6]

The general idea that Australia's PM was out of step with the priorities of the rest of the world weren't assuaged by Obama's headline-grabbing speech at the University of Queensland on 15 November, in which he spoke passionately of the urgent need for action to protect the Great Barrier Reef—which must have come as news to the packed crowd after being so comprehensively assured by the Queensland and federal governments that the reef was actually totally fine and, if anything, could probably do with a bit more dredging spill.

'I have not had time to go to the Great Barrier Reef and I want to come back,' the American president told the Queensland audience. 'I want my daughters to be able to come back and I want them to be able to bring their daughters or sons to visit. And I want that there fifty years from now.'

———

The day before Obama's speech, Abbott got the G20 off to a 'weird and graceless' start, in the words of Bill Shorten, when he chose to use his host's address during the Leaders' Retreat to inspire the most powerful people in the world with stirring oratory about . . . um, how the dumb Australian Senate wouldn't even pass his cuts and extra fees like they knew he wanted.

---

6 According to the *Courier Mail*, Abbott 'muscled up' to Obama on the subject behind closed doors, declaring that 'there could be no effective action on climate change without a strong economy and strongly endorsing fossil fuels'. Sadly, it was not recorded how loudly Obama laughed in Abbott's face at this assertion, which adds to the strong likelihood that this confrontation didn't take place at the G20 so much as in the fevered imagination of one of the prime minister's PR staff, trying to get some of those sweet, sweet pre-shirtfronting poll numbers back.

'It doesn't matter what spending program you look at, it doesn't matter how wasteful that spending program might appear, there are always some people in the community who vote, who love that program very much,' he sighed to a room full of exceedingly busy people who possibly weren't all that interested in spending their very limited time hearing about the domestic political challenges faced by the Coalition.

'For a long time, most Australians who went to see a doctor have been seen at no charge and we would like to see a $7 co-payment for people who are going to see the doctor,' he bafflingly continued. 'In most countries this is not unusual . . . but it is proving to be massively difficult to get this particular reform through the parliament.'

Warming to his theme, and no doubt heartened by the polite smiles of world leaders wondering why they were being bitched to about the Australian Senate when there were inter-national agreements to discuss, Abbott explained that not only had he been prevented from dunning his nation's sick for seeing the doctor, he also wasn't even getting to deregulate universities, thanks to Australia's stupid Democracy-For-Jerks.

'That's going to mean less central government spending and effectively more fees that students will have to pay. We think that this will free up our universities to be more competitive amongst themselves and more competitive internationally, but students never like to pay more.'

While that information was merely irrelevant, Abbott also decided to raise the stakes by boasting about his success in abolishing the carbon tax and emissions trading scheme— material that, it's fair to say, was being presented to the wrong crowd, given the aforementioned US-China emissions trading scheme and Obama's pledge of $US3 billion to create a Global Climate Fund to help poor nations face the costs of climate change.[7]

While there were some positive outcomes from the Brisbane G20, the world noticed Abbott's less-than-stellar job as host. As the international press summed up the weekend's outcomes, the *LA Times* made a point of taking Abbott to task about his address,[8] as did the BBC (also suggesting that the only reason Abbott begrudgingly allowed discussion of climate issues was because Cameron pressured him to do so), while *Times of India* decried Australia's attempts to derail important progress on the subject.

The Australian public, robbed of both a shirtfronting and any serious talk of joining the rest of the world in combating climate change, fell back out of love with the PM. His December approval rating was back in the low thirties. And some of the Cabinet were going from being weaknesses to downright liabilities.

Clearly, it was time to scrape off some barnacles.

---

7   This wasn't lost on Greens leader Christine Milne, who seethed, 'Tony Abbott is showing what a small-minded and insignificant player he is by whining about domestic politics instead . . . It beggars belief that Tony Abbott made a fool of himself, boasting about abolishing an emissions trading scheme in front of a room of people who are committed to taking action on global warming.'

8   Robyn Dixon wrote: 'Occasionally, there's an awkward, pimply youth moment so embarrassing that it does sting. Like when 19 of the world's most important leaders visit for a global summit and Prime Minister Tony Abbott opens their retreat Saturday with a whinge (Aussie for whine) about his doomed efforts to get his fellow Australians to pay $7 to see a doctor. And then he throws in a boast that his government repealed the country's carbon tax, standing out among Western nations as the one willing to reverse progress on global warming—just days after the United States and China reached a landmark climate change deal.'

12

WE ALL LIVE IN A COMPETITIVELY EVALUATED SUBMARINE

In which the captain gets out the barnacle scraper

In November 2014 the defence minister, Western Australian senator David Johnston, wasn't feeling well disposed towards ASC, the shipbuilding company formerly known as the Australian Submarine Corporation.

More specifically, he wanted to ensure that the Port Adelaide-based company would not be getting the contract for manufacturing the fleet of new subs that the government had determined were necessary to keep Australia safe.

'You wonder why I'm worried about ASC and what they're delivering to the Australian taxpayer, you wonder why I wouldn't trust them to build a canoe?' he declared in the Senate, before claiming that the ASC was already $350 million over budget for three air warfare destroyer ships. 'I'm being conservative, it's probably more than $600 million, but because the data is bad, I can't tell you,' he added, scoffing that 'ASC was delivering no submarines in 2009 for $1 billion'.

And thus did one man guarantee the end of his ministerial career.

———

In order to understand how one angry comment sounded the death knell for both the defence minister and, quite possibly, ASC, we need to take a little trip back to the halcyon period before the election when support for Labor, which was just strong enough later on to return to power a seemingly teetering state government, meant some sweet-talking was going to be required by the Coalition in South Australia.

In truth, South Australia was going to get it in the neck once the Coalition got into power. Local television production at the ABC studios would be shut down and the car industry, which had been the state's traditional economic powerhouse, would find its much-needed economic lifeline severed, shutting down manufacturing and the parts industry in the state.[1] Although all that was yet to come, the Coalition was well aware that it needed to be able to offer some sort of kickback to the home state of such Liberal stars as Christopher Pyne and Cory Bernardi. The solution was, as it is in so many situations, a fleet of submarines.

On 8 May 2013 an ebullient Johnston was on the hustings in Port Adelaide, where he was delighted to announce that

———

1   My standard joke about my former home state prior to 2014 was that South Australia's two greatest exports were cars and ambitious people. That joke doesn't work nearly as well now, partly because the car industry has vanished, but also because so many ex-Adelaideans are heading back to enjoy living in an objectively lovely city where they can actually afford to buy a goddamn house.

ASC would have a bright future if the Coalition were to win the election.

'The Coalition today is committed to building twelve new submarines here in Adelaide,' he said to the assembled media. 'We will get that task done, and it is a really important task, not just for the navy but for the nation, and we are going to see the project through . . . as our number-one priority if we win the next federal election.'

That was still the line in September, days before the nation went to the polls, when the Coalition released its defence policy. This stated, in inconvenient black and white: 'We will . . . ensure that work on the replacement of the current submarine fleet will centre around the South Australian shipyards.'

The story had changed a wee bit by the time parliament sat in 2014, when stories started to circulate that the government was inexplicably considering getting its dozen fresh submarines not from ASC, to which it had clearly committed the job, but from Japanese shipbuilding firms.

Johnston's enthusiasm for keeping jobs, defence capacity and public money in Australia had seemingly diminished. In fact, as he explained to the Australian Strategic Policy Institute on 9 April, 'certainly it is desirable that the new submarine would be built in Australia but it is not a blank cheque'.

His explanation as to why the deal had changed was not perhaps the clearest it could be, but boiled down to an implication that the previous government had kept terrible secrets from him, and also the unexpected suggestion that intellectual copyright was really what it was all about in the submarine game.

'It is always difficult for a shadow defence minister to gain a full appreciation on defence planning on account of the necessity for secrecy,' he hedged, 'and as such I placed a caveat on my support; I said at the Defence Debate in Adelaide that "if anything the minister has said is based on fantasy, we'll tell you and we'll revisit this". I have now had extensive discussions with Defence and access to a range of information previously denied me. Notwithstanding, I am still coming to terms with the complexities of intellectual property and our imperative to have sovereign control and proprietorship.'

He gave a more straightforward answer later when a journalist asked if the government was now planning to get Japan to build the subs.

The short answer was yes; the longer one was: 'Well, the Japanese is the nearest design that comes towards what our requirements are. Now, there are no other diesel electric submarines of that size and dimension. It is extremely impressive that they can get a boat of that size, 4200 tonnes with diesel electric power. Obviously, we must be talking to them, and we are, as to what assistance they can provide us with our program going forward and it would be foolish not to ask them.' In other words: also yes, then.

By June 2014 the plan was being presented as a magnificent coup of diplomacy, trade and defence, with foreign minister Julie Bishop explaining: 'Having the Japanese so prepared to discuss not only their technology but even the prospect of purchasing even an entire submarine brings a different flavour to the discussions.'

In August Abbott confirmed that it was all over bar

the shouting for any hope of the subs being built in South Australia, declaring that these sorts of important decisions shouldn't be made on grounds like, for example, whether or not explicit promises were made ahead of a federal election.

'Defence acquisitions have to be made on the basis of defence logic; not industry policy, not regional policy, but on the basis of sound defence policy. I have to stress, we have not yet made a final decision on the design and build of the next generation of Australian submarines. But there will be more of them.' He did insist that: 'The bulk of the Australian work will be done here in Adelaide, and that means more jobs for South Australia.' And it was not lost on anyone that 'bulk of the Australian work' was clearly not the same thing as 'the contracts for the construction'.

In September it was confirmed that Warren King, the head of the Defence Materiel Organisation, had popped over to Japan earlier in the year to have a little chat about what exactly their Soryu submarines were capable of doing.

The following month industry minister Ian Macfarlane was talking up what a boon any submarine contract would be for South Australia, while implicitly acknowledging that they wouldn't be built there.

'Wherever it's built it will have to have the final electronics fitted in Australia,' he explained, 'so there will be extra jobs both in the construction phase and in the maintenance phase. If you've got almost twice as many subs, you've got almost twice as many jobs in terms of looking after them. The real jobs are in the long-term sustaining of the fleet.'

This argument sounded a little like arguing that Adelaide shouldn't be fussed about car manufacturing leaving the state because more cheap imported cars would lead to an employment boom in stereo installation and mag wheel sales. However, there were those who didn't buy the government's line for some reason.

One was South Australian Liberal senator David Fawcett, who was predictably in favour of the subs being built in Australia, explaining: 'It's important to realise that there is nothing available off the shelf at the moment for conventional submarines that is fit for Australia's purpose.'

Fellow South Australian senator Nick Xenophon was also critical—but more because of the lack of transparency of the process, since it looked awfully like the decision had already been made to get Japan to build the things. In response to Abbott's declaration that 'we want the very best submarines and we want them at the best possible price', Xenophon argued: 'You won't be able to do that if you simply have a cosy deal with just one government, namely with Japan.'

And that's the point where Johnston made a formal request for cooperation in a deal with Japan's defence minister, Akinori Eto. The request was made before the Senate Standing Committee on Economics released its report into the future of Australia's submarine fleet, but then again it probably would have made little difference. The majority opinion—put by Labor, Xenophon and fellow independent John Madigan—found that the government should put such contracts to open tender and also prioritise Australian shipbuilders. The government members of the committee, not unexpectedly, disagreed with this conclusion.

As the fight over this report heated up, the defence minister had less and less patience with those who argued that he'd broken an election promise, or that the completely opaque tendering process had been somehow insufficiently transparent. Then, in Senate Question Time on 25 November, South Australian Labor senator Alexander Gallacher asked Johnston a provocative question: 'Why is the minister so intent on breaking his promise to build twelve new submarines in Adelaide that he is now personally denigrating someone who has built and maintained all six Collins-class submarines at the ASC for the past twenty-five years?'

At which Johnston rose to his feet and said the words that lost him his job.

———

Amid the rising chorus of condemnation over Johnston's canoe crack, the PM initially stood by his man.

'He has my full confidence,' Abbott said during Question Time the following day. 'The Minister for Defence is doing an outstanding job, absolutely outstanding job, following six years of neglect by members opposite. It is true the Minister for Defence engaged in a bit of, I think we could say it was a rhetorical flourish, uncalled-for rhetorical flourish, in the Senate yesterday . . . which he didn't mean, which he has withdrawn and he has apologised for.'

And Johnston probably would have weathered the storm, were it not for the timing of the comments. As it turned out, they presented a convenient pretext for the PM to give the man his marching orders.

On 3 December two of the minister's senior staff had been escorted from Parliament House by security on suspicion of leaking embarrassing information to the press following a

News Ltd investigation into the minister's expenses. Johnston and his chief of staff had apparently been 'wining and dining' foreign officials and defence contractors, offering them fancy dinners and nights out, at the very same time as they were cutting defence pay rises to a below-inflation 1.5 per cent.

That revelation was the straw that broke the Lambie's back, with the now-independent Tasmanian senator vowing to vote down every piece of government legislation until defence staff got their full pay rise—a move which all but guaranteed that nothing could pass without the support of either Labor or the Greens.

Johnston wasn't even the biggest failure that the government was wrestling with at the time—the planned university deregulation by education minister Christopher Pyne, the GP co-payment of health minister Peter Dutton and the doomed cuts to welfare of social services minister Kevin Andrews were already doing plenty of damage to the government. This was also when the furore around the conspicuously broken promise of 'no cuts to the ABC and SBS' was at its peak. The PM had made that electoral commitment, but it should have been raining hellfire down on the person responsible, the communications minister—except that Malcolm Turnbull had wisely ensured that the question of job and program losses fell to Abbott rather than himself since the ABC's funding was inarguably being cut.[2]

However, the pay increase dispute guaranteed that Johnston's head would be on the chopping block when the

---

2 Indeed, Turnbull did more than avoid being blamed for ABC cuts; he put the problem square on the PM by admitting that, sure, the 4.9 per cent 'efficiency dividend' was definitely a cut—despite Abbott's semantic attempts to avoid that word.

symbolic bloodletting began a few days later, as the PM announced plans to 'knock a few barnacles off the ship'. In late December Johnston was the only minister to be turfed out of the ministry altogether rather than be shuffled into a new, less embarrassing gig.

Andrews was taken out of Social Services, replaced by immigration minister Scott Morrison—in what was either a promotion to a more high-profile portfolio for a rising star of the government, or an attempt to curb Morrison's leadership aspirations by putting him in a thankless ministry with unachievable expectations, depending on how paranoid you consider the PM to be.

Morrison in turn was replaced by Dutton, whose gift for oratory was better suited to a job where 'no comment' was the default public statement. Dutton's job as health minister was taken by Sussan Ley, immediately doubling the number of non-penis-havers on the front bench.

Andrews was given the Defence portfolio, and it was only weeks before he was to show his mettle before the public when the prime minister authorised a South Australian backbencher to give some good news about the submarine contracts—news which, as it turned out, wasn't entirely true.

———

In February the language around how the submarine tender process would proceed became even more slippery, starting with the announcement that now there was going to be an open tender for the project.

On 8 February South Australian Senator Sean Edwards delightedly announced that ASC absolutely would be able to bid for the gig. No less an authority than Tony Abbott himself had given Edwards the go-ahead to reassure his home state that he had its back; the PM told Chris Uhlmann on ABC *News* that 'you would expect the Australian government to want to get the best product and you would expect the Australian government to give Australian suppliers a fair go'.

Edwards enthused to the media: 'I now call on the management of the ASC and the unions to come together like they never have before and prove that the faith I've had in them through the period from the fourteenth of October when I commenced my lobbying of the PM that they can be the world-class, competitive builder of submarines that they say they can be.'

Why did the PM seemingly have a change of heart? Well, at this point he was facing a leadership spill and was desperately shoring up numbers within the party.[3] Edwards had made his support for Abbott contingent on ASC being able to tender for the submarine contract. And so the PM did what any shrewd leader would do: he took the politically expedient route.[4]

Thus the situation regarding ASC being welcome to bid for the contract changed rather dramatically between the Sunday before the leadership spill motion and the Tuesday after it. Once the spill motion died in the party room on 9 February and the PM's leadership was no longer in doubt,

---

3 All of which will be excitingly explored in one chapters' time. This is more of that foreshadowing, stuff?

4 Interestingly, even SA's somewhat-less-than-critical-of-the-government *Adelaide Advertiser* effectively called bullshit on the offer at the time, by titling its article on this exciting development: 'Prime Minister Tony Abbott promises South Australia chance to tender for future submarines project to win leadership votes'.

the seriousness with which the opinions of South Australian senators was taken had diminished in importance from 'seriously' to 'What, there's a *south* Australia now?'

And thus it became the job of new defence minister Kevin Andrews to, as they put it in management-speak, 'manage expectations'.

———

Andrews fronted the media on 10 February to explain that, despite what Edwards had said, actually, no—there wasn't going to be an open tender but a 'competitive evaluation' that would be 'careful, cautious, [and] methodical'.

Andrews' reputation for quality rhetoric on the fly had taken something of a beating days earlier when he'd pledged his support to 'the government of Tony Abbott and Julia Gillard', and thus it was no surprise that he responded with flustered anger to questions about what precisely was the difference between a 'competitive evaluation' and an 'open tender'. The correct answer, incidentally, was that a 'competitive evaluation' was a made-up term to give the impression of an open process when it was going to be an internal government decision without any of that pesky 'transparency' nonsense. However, that would obviously be an unwise statement to make to the public, and so he took a different tack:

'I'm not going to get into all sorts of definitions and what's a definition and what that is,' declared the man with oversight of our national defence forces. 'I'm saying as the Australian defence minister this is the approach that we are taking.'

That statement was effectively the ministerial equivalent of 'because I said so', with the bonus of suggesting that the minister didn't actually know what he was talking about—or, apparently, what 'definition' meant. Having finance minister Mathias Cormann insist 'there's actually no change in policy' regarding the submarine contracts didn't exactly reassure a public—especially those in South Australia—that was increasingly concerned that the government was making this all up as they went along.

The PM was making a fist of it, envisaging 'a long and bright future for the ASC' and promising that the new submarine contracts would provide five hundred new jobs—but only if ASC was willing to work with the overseas company who'd get the actual gig to build what had now apparently halved and become an order for six Collins-class submarines.

South Australian premier Jay Weatherill called shenanigans, insisting that this was a clear message that a decision had already been made and that the government was 'trying to retrofit a process to bless it. I don't know how you pluck a number like that out of the air. Nowhere in [Abbott's] remarks did he repeat the promise he made at the last election to build twelve submarines here in South Australia.'

South Australia's defence industries minister Martin Hamilton-Smith also pointed out that the terms of the deal, as they were currently understood, guaranteed exactly nothing for the state. 'Nothing short of adhering to the promise that was made to South Australians prior to the federal election that there would be twelve submarines built in Australia, based in Adelaide, will do,' he declared. 'That was the promise the Coalition made, that's the promise that should be kept.'

At the time of writing, whether any shipbuilding or submarine construction will be done in Australia at all is still an open question pending the result of the tend . . . sorry, the competitive evaluation process. France, Germany and Japan had been invited to participate, with the final decision being expected around December 2015.

Meanwhile, in mid-July 2015 ASC announced the sacking of 101 workers.

Then in August 2015, South Australia was again a vitally important state with the government heading down to announce plans to start building a new generation of naval frigates in 2020. Meanwhile Ian Macfarlane announced a bunch of manufacturing grants, with everyone politely sidestepping awkward questions about submarines and the whereabouts of the car industry.

Any suggestion that the trip had been made in a desperate attempt to improve the government's flagging poll numbers (including the projected loss of several lower house seats, including Christopher Pyne's hitherto safe Liberal seat of Sturt) would be both mean-spirited and accurate.

13
THE TERRIBLE, HORRIBLE, NO GOOD, VERY BAD SPILL MOTION

In which the captain faces a ghostly mutiny

The year 2015 dawned bright and bold, amid promises from the prime minister that the discord and gaffes that had characterised the previous three months would be swept aside in a cleansing wave of excellent government. Within weeks he very nearly lost the leadership of his own party.

And it had all started so well, too.

On 14 January Abbott declared he was confident that the GP co-payment would be going ahead, regardless of whether the Senate had indicated any willingness to change their mind on it.

That resolute adherence to policy was shaken somewhat the following day when new health minister Sussan Ley made her presence felt by officially scrapping the planned GP co-payment. She was to subsequently reveal plans to cut the doctors' Medicare rebate by $20—offering GPs the choice of taking a financial hit or passing the cost on to their patients. This was predictably popular with the Australian Medical Association.

The PM's January didn't end well, with the Liberal National Party losing the apparently unlosable Queensland election.[1] Premier Campbell Newman lost his seat and Labor found itself in the unexpected situation of forming minority government under the command of the somewhat surprised-looking Annastacia Palaszczuk.[2]

However, the real clanger was dropped a few days earlier, with the announcements of the Australia Day honours.

———

One of the biggest challenges for any powerful person is to remember to have trusted and respected people around them—people who can look said powerful person in the eye and say, 'No, that's a really stupid idea.'

It's a problem that manifests itself in every area of human activity, perhaps most obviously when a popular band splits up (or goes on, ahem, 'indefinite hiatus'). Typically the first thing that happens is that the members start pumping out their solo albums, full of all the tunes that their bandmates thought were sub-par.

---

1 All right, that's an exaggeration. The ABC's political stats machine Antony Green had called an LNP loss months earlier (and also predicted Newman would lose his seat), but while a Labor swing was predicted it was generally accepted by pundits that the LNP would have enough seats to govern in its own right—which might explain why they didn't think to sweet-talk the independent MPs a little more.
2 It's worth remembering that Queensland is in the unique situation of being a unicameral government (i.e. there's no upper house), so whoever wins has carte blanche over the state. The day I realised this fact was the day when Queensland politics suddenly made sense to me.

'Finally!' the newly minted solo artist thinks. 'I have all these great songs in my back pocket that the other guys just didn't understand. I can hire a new bunch of musicians to realise my glorious vision and finally make a record that perfectly portrays the intricate beauty of my unique personal expression!'

And then the two-star reviews come out, generally followed by a second bitter solo album about how critics are idiots. What follows is a tour of venues a quarter the size of anything the artist's old band played for the last decade, and then a triumphant burying of the hatchets with the announcement of a reunion tour, as everyone realises they're better together than apart—or, at least, better at paying their mortgages.

Never in the history of recorded music has a first solo album transcended the best work of a well-loved band, not least because no-one on a rock star's payroll is going to say, 'Hey, person who can sack me on a whim, that new tune of yours is shit.' There's a reason George Harrison only got two songs per Beatles album, you know.

With this in mind, at some point in the lead-up to the Australia Day honours, Tony Abbott had the following thought: I will give a knighthood to Prince Philip, Duke of Edinburgh.

———

It's not as though the reinstatement of knights and dames to the Australian honours list in 2013 had come without controversy. The move was seen at best to be unnecessary, and at worst to be symbolic of the PM attempting to move Australia back to the Menzies era.

The PM had long made it clear to the nation that he was a staunch monarchist—indeed, between parliamentary gigs in the 1980s he'd been head of Australians for a Constitutional Monarchy, holding the line against the likes of Paul Keating and Malcolm Turnbull as they rang the bell for Australian republicanism. However, giving a knighthood to the husband of Queen Elizabeth II seemed to go beyond mere fanboy excitement, not least because—unlike the other recipients of official honours—it was hard to identify anything that the prince had specifically done for Australia's benefit beyond occasionally turning up.[3]

Presumably Abbott mentioned it to someone in passing. But how did this conversation play out?

Here's my guess:

ABBOTT: So anyway, I've decided to confer a knighthood on Prince Philip.

IMAGINARY STAFFER: . . . I'm sorry . . . Prince Philip?

ABBOTT: Yes.

IMAGINARY STAFFER: As in the husband of the queen? That Prince Philip?

ABBOTT: That's the one.

IMAGINARY STAFFER: Oh. [Pause] And, um, why?

ABBOTT: What do you mean, *why*?

IMAGINARY STAFFER: Well, you look at the other people who are getting honours—like co-Australian of the Year Rosie Batty, who's been a tireless campaigner for domestic violence reform in Australia, or Professor Denis Wakefield for his lifelong work on ocular immunopathology. You're giving him an Order of Australia.

ABBOTT: Yes, and . . . ?

---

3   And let's be honest: isn't turning a prince into a knight technically a demotion?

IMAGINARY STAFFER: Well, I'm just curious as to what Prince Philip has actually, y'know, *done*. Especially as a British citizen of Greek descent who has been in the country, what, half a dozen times?

ABBOTT: Well, he's the prince!

IMAGINARY STAFFER: . . . And?

ABBOTT: And it's about time he got some recognition for his life of service.

IMAGINARY STAFFER: *Recognition?*

ABBOTT: Yes.

IMAGINARY STAFFER: Prince Philip?

ABBOTT: Yes.

IMAGINARY STAFFER: He's already a prince, you realise?

ABBOTT: I do realise that, yes.

IMAGINARY STAFFER: And he's also the Duke of Edinburgh.

ABBOTT: Yes.

IMAGINARY STAFFER: And he's also the Earl of Merioneth, Baron Greenwich, Royal Knight of the Most Noble Order of the Garter, Extra Knight of the Most Ancient and Most Noble Order of the Thistle, Member of the Order of Merit, Grand Master and First and Principal Knight Grand Cross of the Most Excellent Order of the British Empire, Additional Member of the Order of New Zealand, Extra Companion of the Queen's Service Order, Royal Chief of the Order of Logohu, Extraordinary Companion of the Order of Canada, Extraordinary Commander of the Order of Military Merit, Canadian Forces Decoration, Lord of Her Majesty's Most Honourable Privy Council, Privy Councillor of the Queen's Privy Council for Canada, Personal Aide-de-Camp to Her Majesty, Lord High Admiral of the United Kingdom, right?

ABBOTT: Yes.

IMAGINARY STAFFER: And he needs to be given some recognition, you think?

ABBOTT: Look, just send the damn email.

IMAGINARY STAFFER: Rightio then. Anyone else I should know about?

ABBOTT: Well, I'm also thinking we should make Queen
    Elizabeth a dame.
IMAGINARY STAFFER: Let's save that one for 2016, maybe.
ABBOTT: Eh, fine. Hey, how's about Pope Francis?
IMAGINARY STAFFER: Well . . . oh, my phone's ringing, I really
    have to take this.
ABBOTT: I didn't hear anything.
IMAGINARY STAFFER: It's on vibrate.
ABBOTT: Also, a banana isn't actually a phone, is it?
IMAGINARY STAFFER: . . . Yes.

The response to the announcement seemed to take the PM
by surprise.

Bill Shorten was predictably scathing: 'It's a time warp
where we're giving knighthoods to English royalty. Some
people wondered whether it was an Australia Day hoax.'

Northern Territory chief minister and Country Liberal
party leader Adam Giles was even more blue, declaring, 'It
makes us a bit of a joke. It's Australia Day, we're not a bunch
of tossers.'

Even the often-pliant News Corps piled on, with impressively solid jokes about the 'Duke Knight Rises' and scathing
editorials with unambiguous titles like 'Prince Philip's Knighthood Insults All Australians',[4] a tone that carried over to the
report on the actual presentation of the honour by the Duke's
missus, Queen Elizabeth, in April.

Nor was the move beloved by government members
themselves, with Queensland backbencher Andrew Laming

---

4   Shaun Carney didn't mince words in the *Herald Sun*: 'The message in his
appointment was that of the 23 million Australians who rose to celebrate Australia
Day, none bar Air Chief Marshal Houston had contributed to Australia as much as
Prince Philip. That is more than a joke. It is an insult.'

announcing plans to introduce a private members bill to abolish the new honours.

In the end, the PM conceded that he would no longer get to hand out knighthoods and damehoods himself but would have these honours presented by the Order of Australia Council.

Thus the message was sent that the PM's upcoming appearance at the National Press Club was his make-or-break opportunity to make a case for his continued leadership. And . . . well, the 'make' bit didn't exactly happen.

In a speech that made regular and pointed use of the phrase 'the *Abbott* government', there was the predictable rattling of the domestic security cage and a concession that his parental leave plan was now dead in the water. And then he sent a message to his own party: shut the hell up already.

'The Rudd–Gillard–Rudd years cannot become the new normal lest Australia join the weak government club and become a second rate country living off its luck,' he pleaded. 'You elected us to be an adult government focused on you, not on ourselves . . . It isn't a popularity contest . . . You deserve budget repair, no return of the carbon tax, no restart of people smuggling, and no in-fighting . . . Australia deserves the stable government that you elected us to be just sixteen months ago.'

And then the PM left the stage, confident that, with a few petulantly chosen words, he'd secured his leadership within the party.

It must, therefore, have come as an enormous shock to discover that 'b-b-but Labor!' hadn't comprehensively dispelled concerns about his grasp on the leadership. To put it another way: his speech scared the hell out of his marginal seat MPs.

On Tuesday, 3 February, Western Australian backbencher Dennis Jensen announced that the PM no longer had his support—a call echoed by Queensland's Mal Brough.

The following Friday the axe came down: Western Australia's Luke Simpkins called for a spill motion, seconded by another WA MP, Don Randall.

The PM announced that fine, a spill motion would be tabled in the party meeting on Tuesday, 9 February.

And then he brought it forward to a special sitting on the Monday morning.

There are two possible interpretations of this move. One is that he was super-eager to get this over with and get on with the business of government. The other is that this deprived any possible rival from valuable lobbying time: and by 'rival', everyone understood he meant 'Malcolm Turnbull, and possibly Julie Bishop'. That's not least because Turnbull praised the PM for making it a Tuesday meeting about an hour before Abbott's announcement of the change of arrangements.

Bishop was deliberately silent on the topic, but Turnbull conceded that 'if, for whatever reason, the leadership of a political party is vacant then anyone, any member of the party can stand, whether they be a minister or a backbencher, without any disloyalty to the person whose leadership has been declared vacant',[5] which, under the circumstances, was as obvious a statement of intent as if he'd nailed some theses to the door of the PM's office.[6]

---

5 He also described the move of the spill motion from Tuesday to Monday as a 'captain's call', which was a very polite way of saying 'fuck that guy'.

6 Everyone loves a Martin Luther joke, right? That's the sort of insightful, cross-disciplinary gag you can write with an arts degree, kids. Stay in school!

One person who was very clear that he had no intention of making a move was Scott Morrison, possibly because his public rehabilitation from 'guy who ran a mile after that dude was murdered on Manus Island' to 'firm but fair national daddy figure' wasn't yet fully executed—or, more conspiratorially, because he was already having secret negotiations with Turnbull about getting the treasurer gig if there was a leadership change.[7]

The PM had one huge advantage: by convention, everyone in the ministry was obliged to support the leader in the event of a spill motion.

That said, there were a few ministers game to suggest that they had reservations about the current leadership—trade minister Andrew Robb called the concerns of the backbench 'legitimate', while the number of backbenchers willing to put their necks out increased, including high-profile backbenchers Sharman Stone, Warren Entsch and former assistant treasurer Arthur Sinodinos.

Abbott wasn't about to waste time, mind. As mentioned earlier, promises were made to South Australian MPs that if they supported him then the hotly disputed submarine contracts would be opened to bids by local manufacturer ASC, despite the apparent extant promises to Japanese PM Shinzo Abe that his nation would get the gig.[8]

And his efforts worked. Without any challenger emerging to provide an alternative, the spill motion was defeated

---

7   This was purely speculative, it should be made clear, based entirely on the oddly convivial relationship the two factional rivals seemed to have at the time, including very visible Canberra dinner dates at easy-to-photograph outdoor tables. To be fair, summer evenings in the nation's capital are a delight.

8   You know all about this from the last chapter. Fun fact: that tendering process still doesn't seem to be open to South Australian bidders.

61 votes to 39. Of course, if you assume that the ministry voted along the conventional lines, it meant that the overwhelming majority of the backbench wanted change. And even so, a 40 per cent vote for Malcolm Turnbull's shadow was hardly a rousing message of support for the Abbott government.

What was also interesting was that two votes were missing: that of Ross Vasta, who was on paternity leave at the time, and another 'informal' vote: one MP wrote 'pass', perhaps confusing a yes/no vote with the fast money round on *Sale of the Century*.[9]

But Tony Abbott was alive, for now—and ready to claw his way back.

---

9   *Sale of the Century*'s still a thing, right?

14
GOOD GOVERNMENT STARTS TODAY

In which the captain weathers the storm

The leadership spill motion had been defeated, and now it was time to regroup—which, in the tradition of the government, meant that some heads needed a good kicking.

Presumably that's what Tony Abbott was thinking when he fronted the press to declare, 'Good government starts today,' which simply prompted everyone to ask what the merry hell had been going on for the previous near-eighteen months then.

What had just happened raised serious doubts about the capacity of the party's chief whip, Philip Ruddock, whose job, after all, was to prevent it. In his defence, he'd been put into the role effectively as some busy work for a figure too venerable to be shunted into the backbench, but with zero chance of being added to the ministry. However, his failure to stop the backbench from getting uppity resulted in both a professional and personal slight: he was unceremoniously dumped as whip and replaced by Queensland MP Scott Buchholz.

The PM also rewarded South Australian senator Sean Edwards for his support by immediately backing down on his promises regarding submarine construction,[1] but the main thing that was concerning the PM was how he could hold on to his own job.

In fact, without having reached the halfway point of his term, Abbott was already thinking about an early election.

———

It was a turbulent time. The government only had three ministers who seemed to be competent in their portfolios— Julie Bishop, Malcolm Turnbull and Scott Morrison—and all were being touted as potential leaders. Indeed, the afore-mentioned news that Turnbull and Morrison had been dining together in February and March, suggesting an alliance was building between the Man Who Would Be Leader Again and the Man Who Would Be Treasurer And Then Probably Leader A Bit Later, should have been giving Abbott some sleepless nights.

Any doubts about how desperate the prime minister was feeling were extinguished on Tuesday, 17 March, when reports came through that he had canvassed the prospect of calling a surprise double dissolution election during a private dinner he had hosted for key members of his Cabinet. It was a thought bubble, the reports made clear, and not a serious prospect— but the mere fact that the PM was considering it to the point of discussing it with senior colleagues was indicative. As was

---

1 . . . as you learned in chapter 12. See? It all fits together like a *beautiful machine!*

the fact that someone at said dinner was prepared to tell the media about it.

Double dissolutions are the great white whales of Australian politics. They have the mythical power, in the public imagination, to make everything better again by wiping the slate clean. However, like an actual great white whale, they tend to smash everything up. Just ask Captain Ahab.[2]

Double dissolutions are different to simply calling an early election, in that they are full-Senate elections. In a normal election, all of the MPs in the House of Representatives contest their seats, having three year terms, but senators have six year terms and therefore only half of the state senators (plus, for historical reasons, all the senators for the Northern Territory and Australian Capital Territory, as another cruel reminder that they're not proper states) have to go through all that election nonsense at a time.

However, in a double dissolution, everything is up for grabs. This creates unique problems for governments as it becomes easier for independents and micro parties to make it over the line because the required percentage of votes is half that of a normal election. Despite this constitutional ejector seat button being designed for use only in emergencies, and the strong like-lihood these days of any such election packing the Senate with crossbenchers, historically double dissolutions have been used almost exclusively as an excuse to call an early election.

There are a bunch of constitutional conditions that must be fulfilled for a double dissolution, most importantly a 'trigger': a piece of legislation from the House of Representatives that

---

2   Again, kids: stay in school!

either has been rejected twice in the Senate (within no less than three months, but within the same parliamentary session) or been amended in ways that the government will not accept.

There have only been six double dissolutions in the history of the Australian parliament. In exactly one case it worked to the government's advantage—the Liberal-Country government of Robert Menzies was successfully returned with a Senate majority in 1951 after Labor blocked its attempts to denationalise the Commonwealth Bank. Every other attempt has either ended in the government losing the election (the federal Liberal government under Joseph Cook lost to Andrew Fisher's Labor Party in 1914) or being returned without the necessary Senate majority to pass the laws that formed the trigger for the double dissolution in the first place (Gough Whitlam's Labor government in 1974, Malcolm Fraser's Coalition government in 1983, Bob Hawke's Labor government in 1987). And of course there was the Constitutional Crisis of 1975 that saw the Whitlam government dismissed by the governor-general and the Fraser government installed as caretakers before the calling of a double dissolution election. Short version of the impossibly long and complicated story: it didn't end at all well for Whitlam.

———

Fortunately, there was some good news: unlike the elections in South Australia, Victoria or, perhaps most painfully, Queensland, the Coalition had retained New South Wales in the state election of 28 March. There had been a swing against the government of Mike Baird, but not enough to unseat the popular leader. Thus the federal Coalition spent the immediate aftermath of the return of the Baird government by insisting that, sure, it had regularly emphasised throughout the NSW campaign that this was in no way a referendum on the popularity of the federal government but, in retrospect, it totally was. Then again, it was probably not going to start declaring any less-than-flattering truths about the situation, whether historical (traditionally the party that wins the NSW election is the one that loses the subsequent federal one) or purely numerical. Prior to the election there had been rumblings about what a 10 per cent swing against the party would presage for Abbott's leadership. The eventual swing was 9 per cent, which wasn't as bad as it could have been but was still not quite an emphatic vote of confidence.

Baird was a personally popular leader going into the election, but he damn well had to be. The previous few years had been brutal for the Liberals, after the Independent Commission Against Corruption (ICAC) decimated the state front bench and removed Baird's predecessor Barry O'Farrell. His government was facing a backlash over two big issues in the community—coal seam gas mining and the privatisation of electricity assets—and looked set to lose some key regional seats on both scores.

After the comprehensive thumping that the electorate had handed to Labor at the 2011 election, when O'Farrell defeated Kristina Keneally, there was little chance of an immediate comeback for the opposition. Labor's Luke Foley was a new and untested leader, slotted into the job mere weeks before the election and heading a state party that was yet to distinguish itself as being worth the people's vote (and, what's more, had its own ICAC skeletons still rattling around). Yet Labor didn't suffer the bloodbath it should reasonably have expected.

Even with the same Abbott Factor that was assumed to have destroyed Campbell Newman in Queensland, this should have been a cakewalk for the Coalition, and yet the LNP lost fourteen seats to Labor and the Nationals lost Ballina to— of all people!—the Greens. The Greens were the only party that had any genuine reason to celebrate[3] as their Legislative Assembly representation leaped from one to three seats, plus five in the Legislative Council.

Yes, a Labor win would have been a disaster for the PM, but then so would have been an asteroid strike on the Coalition party room—an outcome that was only slightly more likely. But a win's a win, and thus it was an emboldened and resolute government that decided that this first non-sitting week before the release of the budget was a perfect time to have a conversation with Australians about tax.

Specifically, that they should pay more of it.

One of the great unacknowledged things about income tax is that it's a great idea. At least, it's a great idea if you're in favour of things like 'roads' and 'justice systems' and 'hospitals' and 'society not crumbling into a desperate post-apocalyptic *Mad Max* dystopia'.

Our progressive system of taxation also takes a reasonable stab at being somewhat equitable, acknowledging that those at the bottom of the heap are in less of a position to contribute compared with those at the tippity-top. The issue, however, is that income tax is awfully unpopular.

---

3 As well as Ballina, the Greens also picked up the new inner-west seat of Newtown (which was nominally Labor). But you know, it's where all those latte-sipping inner-city types live (please see earlier footnote regarding the author and his café/Macbook/beard policies).

Successive Australian governments and oppositions had ensured that this was the case by demonising tax increases and trumpeting tax cuts for decades, reinforcing the idea that having everyone kick in a bit to keep the nation functioning was an onerous and unreasonable obligation for a citizen to endure. And the problem with having tax cut after tax cut after tax cut is that unless the economy keeps growing exponentially to make up the shortfall, eventually a nation starts running out of money. If said government has also been busily selling off any profitable government-owned entity—such as, say, medical insurer Medibank Private—then the challenge becomes even greater.

While income tax is one big slab of taxation revenue for the government, it's not the only one. Company tax is another, and for a little while it appeared that the government was going to get downright grown-up about it, with Joe Hockey branding corporate tax avoiders as 'thieves' and announcing that he was going to declare war on multinational corporations that sought to minimise their tax burden in Australia. The papers were filled with stories about companies like Ikea and Apple and Google making billions in Australia and paying tax rates that ranged from 'laughable' to 'actually insulting' as Hockey . . . um, went very quiet on the subject, and also reduced funding to the Australian Tax Office. In fact, the ATO lost a staggering 4400 jobs during the first two years of the Abbott government, which had the added effect of making it all but impossible for the office to carry out the sort of investigations that might detect tax-minimisation schemes, much less prosecute them.

However, Hockey's attempt to render the ATO tooth-less hadn't ended there. He also announced that the office shouldn't go bothering the highest-earning companies about their taxes at all, but just let them sort it out themselves. The plan was to introduce an innocuous-sounding cost-saving initiative called the External Compliance Assurance Process, or ECAP. (It was presumably deemed a better name than the equally accurate 'Salute Companies Absconding with Money', or SCAM.) The idea was simple: rather than force the Australian Taxation Office to waste time and resources doing all that pesky 'investigation' stuff, the richest companies would instead be able to work out what tax they should pay via their own external auditors.

Some people—like Labor's Andrew Leigh—suggested that maybe allowing for-profit companies to devolve all their civil responsibilities to other for-profit companies might not in fact be the greatest way to ensure transparency and corporate responsibility. Nevertheless, the pilot was announced in December 2014, with the plan being that it should run for 'three to six months' and see how it shook out.

In March, during an inquiry into tax avoidance by the richest companies and individuals, the government announced another protection for those poor little rich companies with over $100 million in turnover: the seven hundred most profit-able of them would be able to keep their tax records secret in order to prevent—and this is true, please note—their directors and executives being kidnapped by baddies. On 17 March assistant treasurer Josh Frydenberg announced this exciting new strategy, under which tax disclosure laws would be wound back to avoid the apparent epidemic of would-be kidnappers poring over company tax statements on the ATO website, cross-indexing the results with shareholder reports and targeting their wealthy owners with ransom demands.

These changes had been suggested by business owners, naturally because they were terrified for their own safety and definitely not because they were just keen to avoid scrutiny of their accounts. Their panic didn't diminish even when the Australian Federal Police confirmed that they'd heard of exactly zero cases in which this had been suggested, let alone investigated, because it was a beyond-ridiculous notion. Still, the tax records of the wealthy were now off-the-record, and everyone breathed a sigh of relief, confident that nothing supports corporate responsibility like the freedom to act in complete secrecy.

So the conclusion from all of this was that income tax remained electorally unpopular, and corporate tax reform was off the agenda in case all the nation's businesspeople were suddenly kidnapped. But there had to be another alternative—something that brought in more revenue but didn't especially affect the wealthy or in any way hurt the interests of the biggest (and therefore best) of Australia's corporate interests. Something that hit a group less able to hit back would be ideal.

As luck would have it, there was already a perfect alternative.

———

Governments who like to reward the wealthy while not thinking too hard about everyone else have long been fans of the notion of flat taxes. By this mechanism all people pay the same, regardless of whether they can afford it or, importantly, can afford a hell of a lot more. And it makes a certain amount of sense, provided that one's notion of fairness is predicated on the same principles of equality that govern six-year-olds—that one should always insist on having more ice-cream than anyone else.

—

As previously pointed out,[4] flat taxes disadvantage those at the bottom more than the wealthy. Thus it came as no surprise that Joe Hockey decided to release at the end of March the Treasury's new 'Re:think' white paper on taxation with the announcement that he wanted to have a national conversation about raising the Goods and Services Tax.

The argument contained within the paper was straight-forward enough: government revenue took a hit during the Global Financial Crisis because people were inconveniently failing to earn nice taxable incomes, and the growing size of the ageing and retiring population was going to put a further brake on things as this required government spending to continue to rise. Clearly we had to do something other than rely on income and company taxes, so . . . oooooh, how's about we whack up the GST a bit, huh?

It was a magical moment, not least because it finally gave the government a clean sweep on reversing literally every-thing that Abbott had declared in his notorious declaration of September 2013 on SBS News.[5] Cuts to health? Check! Cuts to education? Check! Changes to pensions? Boom! Cuts to the ABC and SBS? Oh, checkity-check-check! And now: proposed changes to the GST.

---

4   It was back in chapter 9, just in case you're flipping through this book or reading it in an unconventional non-chronological order. And if so, good for you: don't let The Man tell you what order to read your non-fiction! Boom! Fight the power!
5   See chapter 1, if you need to be reminded of this piece of Fabulous Fibsmanship.

It was also an ambitious suggestion, given that almost five months earlier the treasurer had faced threats of a revolt by Western Australian backbenchers for even suggesting an increase in the GST. A letter, signed by seven MPs and two senators from that state, had been sent to the media on 13 November 2014, asking that WA's GST revenue be upped from thirty cents in the dollar to seventy-five. That, oddly enough, hadn't gone down well with the feds. Premier Colin Barnett was to go even further on 9 April, raising the ever-popular spectre of secession—or, at least, the somewhat opaque 'non-cooperation', according to his treasurer, Mike Nahan—if the state didn't get a larger cut of the tax. He called it their 'Boston Tea Party moment'.[6]

However, the selling of the GST to the electorate was to kick into gear later in the year—first there was Joe Hockey's second budget to release!

———

The main response to this budget was relief, followed by surprising—indeed, inexplicable—degrees of praise.

The budget itself was dubbed the 'Morrison Budget', so certain was the press that the social services minister had softened it. That people saw the gentler budget and suspected Morrison's hand—the same ol' softie who had held asylum seeker children on Christmas Island as bargaining chips unless the Senate agreed to allow him to make sweeping changes to the immigration laws, including the removal of all references

---

6   Of course, since the state was struggling because the price of iron ore—which had been buoying the local economy to marvellous effect—had bottomed out, it's hard to see how it would have kept itself afloat as an independent nation. Also, what would it call itself? West Not-Australia? Newer Zealand?

to that pesky 1951 Refugee Convention that Australia was a signatory to and of which all its asylum seeker policy was unambiguously in breach—said volumes about the public perception of the tender hearts beating within the chests of Joe Hockey and finance minister Mathias Cormann.

There were few of the savage cuts of the previous year, and no talk of the debt-and-deficit disaster that had necessitated the previous year's harshness—which was a nice surprise, but was also nakedly political, because it sure as heck wasn't because the economy was heading to surplus.

In fact, the deficit—which had been such a terrifying problem in 2013, at a nightmarish four-year forward estimate of $54.6 billion, according to the Pre-Election Economic and Fiscal Outlook report released by Treasury under Labor—had now blown out to an eye-watering $123 billion, according to the Mid-year Economic and Fiscal Outlook Hockey and Cormann had released in December 2014. That second number, you might notice, is larger than the first.

However, that wasn't apparently a worry—as Hockey assured the nation, just as soon as growth went back to previous levels, things would bound along to surplus. Indeed, the Reserve Bank's decision to drop interest rates to near-historic lows of 2 per cent in May was spun by the treasurer not as a worrying indictment on the state of the sputtering economy but as a golden opportunity to get out and borrow money while it was so wonderfully cheap.

This was excitingly at odds with his attitude in 2013 when the Reserve Bank had cut interest rates by a quarter of a per cent to 2.5. At the time Hockey had declared that this was clear evidence of an emergency created by Wayne Swan's profligacy and that the Reserve's decision was 'not because the economy is doing well, it's because the economy is deteriorating'. That negative message was gone in 2015, along with warnings about the perils of ballooning personal and business debt. Such doomsaying had now been replaced with excitement about the benefits of ballooning personal and business *opportunity*!

'Now is the time to borrow and invest . . . in the things that help to create jobs,' a jubilant-looking Hockey told reporters. 'This interest rate cut will help to facilitate those green shoots—it's as much about putting fertiliser on the green shoots as anything else.'

To be fair, bullshit is a genuinely excellent fertiliser.

———

Of course, there were still a few teensy tiny problems. One was that the budgetary projections being made were, at best, profoundly sanguine—not to say downright delirious.

For one thing, they were based on the assumption that all the savings flagged in the 2014 budget had been passed, which, as you've probably noticed at this point, they had largely not. And there was the whole deficit-doubling thing. And the assumption that the export price for coal wouldn't drop below $45 a tonne (at the time of writing it was heading to $40 as China slashed its imports of thermal coal).

Had that not been enough dubious assumptions, there was the further one that growth in Australia would somehow clamber back to the 3.5 per cent that Hockey explained would get Australia back on track to a surplus, and which everyone from the International Monetary Fund to the Reserve Bank considered somewhere between 'optimistic' and 'delusional'.

But that was a tomorrow problem! The Abbott government was on a roll and nothing—not its own rhetoric, not economic reality, not the Human Rights Commission bleating about treatment of asylum seekers[7]—was going to slow it down!

Except ... well, then some weird things happened just when the PM's popularity seemed on the rise. One was because of what came out of Abbott's mouth, and the other was because of what went into it.

The first bit was in relation to remote Aboriginal communities—specifically, ones in Western Australia that were, in the opinion of the state government, 'unviable'. The argument was that, as the federal government had announced it would no longer be funding essential services to remote communities and would instead be shifting all those costs back to the states after a one-off payment, the WA budget didn't have enough in its coffers to keep all of these 274 small places serviced with roads and police and other such fripperies. Thus the government would shut between 100 and 150 of them down and relocate the residents to larger towns.

It wasn't lost on anyone that the handful of settlements earmarked for closure were, according to the leaks, exclusively Aboriginal. This suggested that the small communities settled by non-Indigenous folks were to be miraculously spared from this purely-motivated-by-economic-reality-that's-for-darn-sure cull.

There was also the point, which was no doubt a whimsical coincidence, that some of the places to be closed down just so happened to be in regions thought to contain large mineral

---

7   More foreshadowing!

deposits, and that mining companies would very much like to have a bit of a fossick around there without all that time-consuming and expensive Native Title stuff that normally had to be negotiated with the traditional owners of the land. And—again, purely by coincidence, of course—there was the fact that one of the conditions of Native Title was demonstrating an 'unbroken connection to the land', which might be tricky for said traditional owners if they've been forced to relocate an inconvenient two hundred kilometres away.

Finally there was a point made most clearly by Indigenous leader Noel Pearson, one of the PM's most regular advisers: at the risk of suggesting that maybe racism was a thing in Australia—why, *perish the very thought!*—there was a chance that, just maybe, folks in country towns wouldn't be unambiguously welcoming of these forcible new arrivals.

'Who is going to welcome these people in the country towns and suburbs of this country,' Pearson asked bluntly, 'as if there's a big welcoming mat for Aboriginal people from remote communities to be welcomed into the social and economic mainstream of Australia?'

WA premier Colin Barnett tried very, very hard to win over the public—even going to all the trouble of spreading misleading stories about epidemic levels of STI infection from sexual abuse among remote youth, which were inconveniently revealed to be false.[8]

---

8 In fact, remote communities *do* have higher rates of STIs—especially gonorrhoea—but there's no evidence that it's because of child sexual abuse and plenty of evidence that it's because of adolescents having sex. So it's more of an access to health services issue than a criminal justice one. (To be fair, the exact same disease=abuse strategy had worked wonders in getting the Howard government to impose the Northern Territory's 'intervention', based on similarly invented evidence.)

Now, this was a difficult question and one that required tact and discretion—or, at the very least, a total shifting of the blame to the Western Australian government and not making any comment at all. After all, Abbott had made clear in the run-up to his election that he planned to be the First Indigenous PM, who was committed to spending his first week in office in a remote community![9] So it was a little unexpected for Abbott to essentially blame the communities themselves.

On 11 March, the PM took the opportunity of a radio interview to explain: 'It's the job of the taxpayer to provide reasonable services in a reasonable way. Indeed to provide high-quality services in a reasonable way. What we can't do is endlessly subsidise lifestyle choices if those lifestyle choices are not conducive to the kind of full participation that Australians should have.'

Oddly enough, describing living on traditional land as being a 'lifestyle choice' didn't go down at all well.

Shorten immediately demanded that the PM apologise for his comments, but a rather more strident response came from Warren Mundine, chair of Abbott's Indigenous Advisory Council, who threw down on Radio National: 'These people are actually living on their homelands and it affects a lot of

---

9   The promise was made on 10 August 2013, a month before the election, and what Abbott said exactly was this: 'Why shouldn't I, if you will permit me, spend my first week as prime minister—should that happen—on this, on your country? Why shouldn't the prime minister of our country, and why shouldn't the senior officials of our country, be prepared to devote a week a year—just one week—to an overwhelming focus on the issues of Indigenous Australia? Surely that is not too much to ask of our government, of our prime minister, of our senior officials.' Needless to say, this grand suggestion wasn't acted on. Abbott did, however, visit a lot of remote communities during 2014 and 2015, and spent a grand total of four days in Arnhem Land in September 2014, a year after gaining office. And yes, no other PM has spent a week in Arnhem Land either—but then again, none has ever specifically promised they would do so while on the campaign trail immediately before they were elected.

things, it affects their cultural activities, it affects their Native Title, it affects a number of areas. It's not as simple as . . . if someone from Sydney decides to have a tree-change and go and live in the bush. It's about their life, it's about their very essence, it's about their very culture.'

Pearson was even more scathing: 'I think it's a very disappointing and hopeless statement by the prime minister, quite frankly,' he told ABC Radio's *The World Today*. 'He has got no plan for the future of these communities in the event that they close down. And I'm just bitterly disappointed to hear this deranged debate go on in the substandard manner in which it's being conducted.'

Abbott kept on message when talking to Alan Jones a few days later: 'If you or I chose to live in a very remote place, to what extent is the taxpayer obliged to subsidise our services and, I think, this is a very real question,' he said, incorrectly. 'It is incredibly difficult for the kids to go to school, if there's only half a dozen of them, and getting teachers there is all but impossible. Similarly, it's very difficult for the adults to get a proper job if there's no employment within hundreds of miles and this is where we have to be a little bit realistic.'

Joe Hockey agreed, seemingly implying that those in remote communities were probably just making up excuses to stay put. 'Do they want that lifestyle to live in a remote area? Some of them do. Some of them say it is part of their tradition.'

Julie Bishop stopped short of assuring reporters than some of the PM's best friends were Aboriginal, declaring: 'The prime minister is deeply concerned about Aboriginal matters. He has shown his deep passion and interest for many years.'

There was another misstep with the PM's video message for St Patrick's Day, which was judged to be spectacularly patronising. Irish groups took issue with his linking of Irish culture with binge drinking while others took issue with the fact that he had basically repeated the message he had delivered the year before, from referencing the green tie he was wearing to using the same tired line about having 'a Guinness or two, or maybe even three'. But that was just a prelude to what was without doubt the oddest moment of his career.

———

Deciding to live in economically disadvantaged Tasmania was definitely not a lifestyle choice—and that's why the prime minister was happy to pop down and announce a special $60 million grant for Tasmania's farmers, to help make their projects economically sustainable (although they should have thought of that *before* they chose to put their lifestyles there and started expecting handouts, surely?).

In any case, as he was being shown around Devonport's Charlton Farm Produce by proprietor David Addison on 14 March, the PM picked up a brown onion and bit into it like an apple.

It wasn't even peeled.

Addison, who works with onions and therefore might be assumed to be across the many ways in which the things are eaten, was taken aback at this exciting new method of onion-consumption. Because—and it's difficult to overemphasise how odd this is—*the Prime Minister of Australia picked up and ate an unpeeled onion.*

'I may have said "it's a shame they weren't peeled" and he

just started eating it,' Mr Addison told reporters, who were as dumbfounded as he was. 'It was just spontaneous and there weren't even any tears.'

It was a small thing, but it sent a strong message. And that message was: 'I don't really know what you people do on this planet, but where I come from onions is what we eat, peel and all, and we don't cry.'

Perhaps it was coincidence, but this was the point at which the polls started to drift against the PM again.

Presumably he comforted himself with a bushel of onions.

15
I'M A FIXER

In which one of the captain's most trusted crewmen runs the ship aground

Australia benefited greatly from congealing at the same time that the better-established European societies were busily getting on with the Enlightenment, which included the idea that crime was a product of ignorance, and that ignorance could be eliminated by education.

It was a big change from the general notion that school was a wasteful indulgence, since children were expected to fill the gap left by their parents once they dropped dead. Sure, universities existed, but they were less centres of higher learning than just more expensive hangouts for the sons of the wealthy to cool their heels before taking over Daddy's fortune.[1]

---

1 David Hunt's magnificent *Girt: An Unauthorised History of Australia* depicts this era well, with Joseph Banks's time at Eton and Christ Church College characterised as being spent among fellow scions of the wealthy, torturing animals (including chasing a 'ham-strung ram' through the streets) and learning how to smoke. Indeed, it appears that Banks's capacious intellect developed in spite of, rather than as a result of, his time in Oxford.

Australian universities started appearing in the mid-1800s (the University of Sydney was first, in 1850) and schooling started to become compulsory, if not especially well-enforced, in the 1870s. So we've long been informed by the notion of the desirability of education and the government having responsibility for ensuring its provision.

Of course, there were rumblings from both the rural and moneyed classes along the lines of 'Why should a blacksmith's son get his head filled with this nonsense, if he's just going to be a blacksmith?', but by and large Australians assumed that a smart, highly skilled populace was a prerequisite for an informed liberal democracy. So it was something of a surprise when the Abbott government looked at the state of tertiary education and went, 'Say, why are we educating all these blacksmiths, exactly?'

———

As in much of the rest of the world, Australian universities were expensive luxuries for the wealthy classes until around the middle of the twentieth century. After World War II governments realised the leaps forward in science and technology that war had wrought might be handy things to apply in peacetime, and that the jobs of the increasingly industrialised world required more and more qualifications and training.

Research was deemed so important that the Commonwealth government created the research-only Australian National University in Canberra with a view to becoming a Harvard-style centre of excellence, and by the late 1950s the desire to improve standards across the nation's institutions saw the federal government take control of university funding away from the individual states.

There was a flurry of uni building in the sixties[2] and seventies, and then in 1973 the Whitlam Labor government abolished university fees, making tertiary education a right for all Australians who had the school results to justify a place.

That golden age didn't last too long. The Coalition government of Malcolm Fraser changed the funding model in 1975 and by the mid-eighties fees were creeping back in, eventually resulting in the Higher Education Contribution Scheme (HECS) and subsequently the Higher Education Loan Program (note the cruelly ironic acronym, HELP).

While Labor has long ago abandoned the notion of free universities, it's really been the conservative side of politics that has battled against this idea the most vigorously, led by powerful politicians wielding the economic and social advantages conferred by their free universal tertiary education. Among those fortunate beneficiaries was one Christopher Maurice Pyne (Bachelor of Laws, University of Adelaide; Graduate Diploma of Legal Practice, University of South Australia), whose job as education minister in the Abbott government was a simple one: deregulate universities, allowing them to set their own fees to make up the shortfall left by government cuts to tertiary funding. The fact that the mid-to-well-paying jobs of the future all appeared to require at least an undergraduate degree only added to the government's enthusiasm—why, this just meant demand would be even higher, surely?

---

2   Shout out to Flinders University of South Australia, home to glorious brutalist architecture, my genuinely terrible philosophy honours thesis, and a pond that is home to the most entitled ducks in the entire tertiary education sector. Seriously, Flinders undergrads, if you settle down pondside for a relaxing pre-tutorial breather, your lunch will be forfeited. Consider yourself warned.

Sure, there was an argument that increasing the cost of education would price it out of the reach of the people who would benefit most from the poverty-escaping tools of higher education. Also, there was the fact that Pyne was embarking on a mission to effectively privatise the sector at the exact same time that the United States was looking at the effects of its own privatised higher education sector—particularly the trillion-plus dollars of accumulated student debt, much of which even the most optimistic observers conceded was never going to be recovered—and going, 'This is obviously a situation we should address before it collapses the nation's economy.'[3]

And sure, there were people asking questions like: 'Won't it be hard for young people to begin their professional lives saddled with a mortgage-sized debt—not least because that will, for example, make it harder for them to get actual mortgages?'

However, the important thing to keep in mind about such questions is that they were largely not about privileged students whose parents could afford the upfront fees, and therefore didn't involve demographics with which Pyne or the rest of the front bench were familiar, let alone interested in.

———

Ahead of the election the Coalition was at pains to insist it was on a 'unity ticket' with Labor on education funding generally. It was, we were assured, eager to implement the Better Schools Plan, based on the recommendations of the *Review of Funding for Schooling* report which had been produced by a panel under the chairmanship of David Gonski.

---

3   At the time of writing, US student debt had ticked over the US$1.2 trillion mark. So, y'know, definitely something that Australia should seek to emulate.

Thus there was a predictable outcry when Pyne had a change of heart once he got into the ministerial seat and decided that, nah, he wasn't a fan of the report and didn't fancy implementing its recommendations after all.

'I will renegotiate all funding agreements with the signatory and non-signatory jurisdictions, as well as the Catholics and the independents, to ensure that they are fair and equitable to everyone within the funding envelope that Labor promised,' he pontificated in November. 'I'm not going to proceed with a school funding model that is inequitable and utterly incomprehensible.'

He was forced to abruptly reverse that mere weeks later, although he still only agreed to fund four of the six years planned.[4] After all, Pyne was not about to respect the decisions of the previous education minister—one Bill Shorten. He had some exciting new ideas of his own.

Before we follow the tumultuous journey of Pyne's legislative shipwreck, it's worth looking at what exactly was being proposed and what the justifications for this might have actually been. Essentially the idea was that the current funding model—in which universities were heavily subsidised by the federal government, which exerted some control over the fee structure—was 'unsustainable' and therefore had to

---

4 It's worth noting that the states had signed off on the Gonski Report before the change of government and were less than thrilled by Pyne's stated intention of killing off its recommendations. Most strident was NSW education minister, the National's Adrian Piccoli, who pledged in November 2013 that he would hold Pyne to his promise to implement its recommendations. He repeated his intention to pursue the Gonski reforms as recently as March 2015, when he took issue with Victoria's new education minister, Labor's James Merlino, for appearing to back away from the national agreement. With the NSW state government increasingly being seen as the gold standard for the LNP, Piccoli was a bad enemy for Pyne to make.

be freed up to allow unis to set their own fees for Australian students. International students had always had to pay fees to attend Australian universities, but one issue for universities—particularly the prestigious Group of Eight[5]—was that the lucrative flow of international students looked like it was beginning to slow to a drip. Countries like China and India had been investing heavily in education and developing their own high-quality institutions in the hope of stemming the brain drain of their smart young people to Western countries like Australia. Thus there was support for the government's plan from the majority of the nation's vice-chancellors, who saw a possible improvement in their income stream. But it was liked by no-one else. Academics hated it, seeing it as a barrier to access for people looking to study. Students hated it, fearing a greater financial burden than they were already enduring under the HECS system. And the public hated it because they didn't want to be supporting their children to the tune of tens of thousands of extra dollars in order to save them carrying a six-figure debt when they graduated.

———

Pyne wasn't merely concerned with the parlous state of higher education, mind; he was also deeply worried about the children.

While schools were technically a state responsibility, their reliance on Commonwealth funding meant that there was still

---

5 The Group of Eight consists of the Australian National University, Monash University, the University of Sydney, the University of Adelaide, the University of New South Wales, the University of Melbourne, the University of Queensland and the University of Western Australia. The group is not to be confused with the Gang of Four, not least because they're neither considered to have committed treason against the Chinese Communist Party during the Cultural Revolution, nor performed angular New Wave punk-funk in the UK from the late 1970s onward.

room for the minister to throw his weight around. And thus it was that in January 2014 Pyne announced an inquiry into whether there was a 'leftist bias' in schools. Or, rather, to investigate that there was a bias, *obviously*, and that it needed fixing.

To that end, one of those appointed to investigate this urgent issue was Kevin Donnelly—a man whose deep impartiality on the subject was perhaps best illustrated by his ranting about how modern teaching was poisoned by a 'subjective' view of culture, which caused terrorism and neglected the Judeo-Christian values that he insisted were at the core of all Australian institutions.[6] Donnelly was perfect for the job, since he was head of the Education Standards Institute, an organisation funded (as the *Guardian* discovered) by the K Donnelly Family Trust and which railed against the 'Indigenous, Asian and environmental' perspective taught in Australian schools. He also warned that the leftists were determined to teach kids to be gay, writing in *The Punch*: 'Government and other faith-based schools will also be made to teach a curriculum that positively discriminates in favour of gays, lesbians, transgender and intersex persons.'[7]

---

6   That might sound ludicrous—but that was his claim in a piece published in *The Australian* on 19 June 2013 entitled 'PM's School Report Flawed': 'The civics curriculum argues in favour of a post-modern, deconstructed definition of citizenship . . . The flaws are manifest. What right do Australians have to expect migrants to accept our laws, institutions and way of life? Such a subjective view of citizenship allows Islamic fundamentalists to justify mistreating women and carrying out jihad against non-believers.' You know, because pretty much all domestic terrorists were students of history and the arts, right?

7   Donnelly also worked for tobacco giant Philip Morris, developing an educational package for kids teaching them to make their own decisions. The 'I've Got the Power' program didn't explicitly say, 'Hey, kids, are you going to let your parents and so-called "doctors" tell you not to enjoy the smooth, rich taste of Philip Morris tobacco products?', but it certainly didn't avoid it.

Having established that maybe he needed another voice to complement that of the self-professed head of a self-invented standards bureau, who sees Asian and gay bias lurking around every corner, Pyne also appointed Ken Wiltshire: a man who had called the implementation of the Gonksi reforms by the Gillard government 'a national disgrace' (although, it should be added, he supported the recommendations of the report) and had railed against Gillard forming a minority government on the basis that 'Through this back door Labor would be able to introduce the Greens' priorities on gay marriage, softer border protection, and heftier mining taxes and so on.'[8]

So, again, this was a man who knew on which side his ideological bread was buttered[9]—even though he was forced to distance himself from his colleague when Donnelly took to the airwaves to argue that schools should absolutely reintroduce corporal punishment, because he'd found it 'very effective' when his physical education teacher had beaten students up back in his own school days.[10]

The report was delivered in October 2014, and found precisely what it was intended to find: that, oh, there was so much leftie bias being taught to the nation's precious, precious children.

---

8   'On all counts, Coalition deserves independents', Australian, 6 September 2010.
9   The resolutely heterosexual side, clearly.
10 On 2UE on 16 July 2014 he said: 'Whenever there were any discipline problems [his phys ed teacher] would actually take the boy behind the shed and say, "We can either talk about this or you can throw the first punch." That teacher would probably lose his job now but it was very effective. He only had to do it once and the kids were pretty well behaved for the rest of the year.'

But this was just a side dish to the meal that Pyne was making of university funding changes—changes that weren't going down at all well.

———

In May 2014 the nation had reacted to the education component of the federal budget with genuine surprise: a $1.1 billion cut in funding, a 20 per cent increase in student contributions to education, and the deregulation of fees for universities— with 20 per cent of said fees being earmarked for university scholarships.

The general response by experts was that no-one seemed to really know what the effect of deregulation of fees would be, beyond the forlorn hope that perhaps the scholarships would offset the number of students who'd be unable to go to uni for fear of open-ended debts.

In August Pyne laid out more specifics, which included a 20 per cent funding cut, deregulation of fees, upping the interest rate on student loans to CPI levels, dropping the income threshold below which repayments were no longer required, removal of the 25 per cent loading on non-Commonwealth-subsidised HELP students and a cut in funding for the Research Training Scheme, which would be covered by universities charging doctoral students.

'Given the scale of costs now present in the higher education system, it is time students picked up a fairer share of the tab for these interest charges,' Pyne insisted with a straight face. 'It's a good deal. It's the best deal an Australian will ever get'—a bold claim to make, given the deal that had existed at the time when Pyne and his colleagues had been undertaking their own studies.

Pyne was bullish about the chances of his legislation passing, despite the fact that it was definitely not going to do so. Sure, Clive Palmer had already instructed his party to knock back the reforms, thereby ensuring that, without Green and/or Labor support, it couldn't pass, but Pyne was inexplicably chipper about it in an interview on ABC TV's *7.30* on 6 August.

'Well I don't think he's ever said that he is going to vote against our higher education reforms. He has been very careful to say he wants to have free education, in fact, but I think Clive realises that neither the Liberal Party nor the Labor Party will vote in favour of free education because obviously we can't afford it. But he hasn't as yet said that he's against our higher education reforms. Now he has said he's against other things that the government is proposing to put through the Senate, so I do take heart from the fact that if you haven't said no, then we're a long way from ending the siren, as they say.'[11]

Except there was one teeny tiny little thing that happened in that interview . . .

Pyne was in typically upbeat form as he chatted with Sarah Ferguson about how the reforms were absolutely going to pass the Senate, because they were great. But a bit of a cloud passed over his face when Ferguson explained how Bruce Chapman, the man described as 'the architect of HECS', had flagged concerns about how higher upfront costs and larger post-study debts would disadvantage low-income earners generally and

---

11 Pyne was wrong: no-one says 'ending the siren'. Not even the shadowy, mysterious 'they'.

women in particular, since men typically earned more and therefore were able to pay off their debts faster.

Well, Christopher wasn't having that.

'I don't accept it because what will happen at universities is that vice-chancellors and their leadership teams will know that they should not charge and will not charge higher fees for courses which are typically going to be studied by people who'll be nurses and teachers and therefore not earn high incomes over a period of time,' he blithely explained.

'Now, women are well-represented amongst the teaching and nursing students. They will not be able to earn the high incomes that, say, dentists or lawyers will earn, and vice-chancellors in framing their fees, their fee structure, will take that into account. Therefore the debts of teachers and nurses will be lower than the debts, for example, of lawyers and dentists.'

When Ferguson asked how this would affect female lawyers and dentists who had racked up debts and then taken time off to start families, Pyne waved away her concerns and moved on to other details of the plan.

But the damage was done. There was a predictable outcry from people who thought his argument that women don't get high-powered degrees was a) demonstrably false, and b) not exactly an argument for why gender inequality was a win for the ladies.

The legislation went to parliament on 28 August and, despite Pyne's relentless optimism, was immediately killed in the Senate.

In September his helpful statement scored him the 2014 Ernie Award, the annual celebration of the nation's Top

Sexists.[12] Normally the Silver Ernie is reserved for politicians, but Pyne managed to win both the Gold and Silver awards for the one comment.[13] That's an achievement, technically.

———

By January 2015 the language had changed again: Pyne needed to make the cuts because, predictably, of Labor. 'The reason we have to do this reform of universities is because Labor cut $6.6 billion from universities over the course of their government,' he explained, making the interesting case that the cuts were necessary because . . . um, there had been cuts.

This was also a load of tosh: Labor had actually increased funding for tertiary education over the Rudd/Gillard/Rudd era; according to former education minister Kim Carr, funding rose 'from $8.1 billion in 2007 to $14 billion in 2013' with an increase in student numbers, although that was also accompanied by increased student contributions (though, technically, that wasn't a university funding issue per se).[14]

Now there was a new deal on the table: Pyne declared that he'd negotiate on the $1.9 billion in cuts to university funding,

---

12 The Ernies are named for Ernie Ecob, former secretary of the Australian Workers Union, who insisted in 1989: 'Women aren't welcome in the shearing sheds. They're only after the sex.' So the Ernies certainly uphold a proud legacy of Australian feminist thought.

13 Other winners that year included Kyle & Jackie O, for cleverly asking a sports journalist on air if she'd slept with cricketers. Abbott took out the Clinton award for repeat offenders for a record-breaking eighth year.

14 Why was Pyne's $6.6. billion nonsense? Several reasons: a) it takes into account 'forward estimates' up to 2016–17, rather than the period Labor was actually in power; b) Labor's proposed 2013 $2.3 billion cut—sorry, 'efficiency dividend'— never got passed, and was disowned by the party under Shorten in any case; and c) not all those increased student contributions were implemented. Labor did also convert student scholarships to loans, which technically saved $1.2 billion, if you assume that they eventually get paid back. Still rather a dick move, though.

provided that the Senate just deregulated fees already: 'We are committed to these reforms . . . and we will negotiate with the crossbenchers and do whatever needs to be done.' And there was a bonus threat: either the Senate agreed to the cuts or he'd yank $150 million in funding from the National Collaborative Research Infrastructure Strategy, a Labor-established scientific research initiative between industry, government and the research sector that had barely anything to do with universities.

'There are consequences for not voting for this reform and that's very important for the crossbenchers to understand,' Pyne told Barrie Cassidy on the ABC's *Insiders*. 'The consequences are that potentially 1700 researchers will lose their jobs.'

It was a brave move to argue that those job losses would be something other than Pyne's decision, since this move now looked less like negotiation and rather more like blackmail.

The Senate appeared to conclude that arbitrarily removing money from an entirely unrelated department was a bad look for the government and all but dared Pyne to have a go if he thought he was tough enough. The former Palmer United senators were particularly scathing, with Glenn Lazarus issuing a statement that read: 'Australians should be angry that the Abbott government is threatening to hurt people by cutting more jobs, including research and scientific positions, in order to try and blackmail the Senate into supporting deregulation . . . This is disgusting behaviour and demonstrates the appalling ethics of this government.'

Jacqui Lambie, meanwhile, had been in hospital—but she left her sickbed for the express purpose of being in parliament to vote against the legislation, declaring: 'Mr Pyne will need more than just a Kleenex I offered him at the start of this debate for the political pain I'm about to cause him.'

Independent Nick Xenophon was no less caustic: 'This is not the way to negotiate with the Senate. It is reckless, it is irresponsible.'

Pyne backed down, telling the Senate that, fine, the NCRIS funding would remain and he'd find the money elsewhere. Now, just please pass the damn legislation.

On 17 March the plans were given the slap-down, with Labor, the Greens and five-eighths of the Senate crossbench giving it a comprehensive 'nup'.[15]

Despite this second slap-down, Pyne put on a brave face for his chat with Sky News, in what was one of the more memorable interviews of his storied public life.

When David Speers asked how he'd managed to prevent the closure of the NCRIS, despite not getting his savings through, Pyne spoke over him: 'I've fixed it. I'm a fixer.'

'How did you fix it?'

'I've fixed it by funding it in another way which you'll find out in the budget,' Pyne responded with a tight grin.

'Why can't you tell us?' Speers asked.

'I want it to be a surprise for you.'

The playfulness became a bit more strained as Speers asked where exactly that money was coming from, with Pyne shooting back: 'That's really not your concern.'

---

15 For the record, the senators in favour of the change were ex-DLP-turned-Indpendent John Madigan, Family First's Bob Day and Liberal Democrat David Leyonhjelm. You probably didn't need to use your surprised face in response to that information.

'Well, it's taxpayers' money, Minister,' Speers pointed out.

'Well, it will be clear in the budget,' Pyne replied.

Oddly enough, as the 2015 budget revealed, there were no such savings to be found. Indeed, not only was there no saving to be seen, there was at least one hidden cost in there: the budget appeared to assume that fee deregulation was going to kick in as of 1 January 2016.

That seemed . . . let's go with 'ambitious'.

———

By this stage even the chancellors of the Group of Eight—including Pyne's alma mater, Adelaide University—had decided they'd had enough of waiting for the minister to deliver on his promises.

These universities had, unsurprisingly, been loudly in favour of fee deregulation. Obviously, they figured that uni funding was unlikely to increase and that their history and prestige would make them desirable commodities—unlike the lesser, grubbier universities muddying up the sector which, for the most part, argued that a) fees were a morally repugnant idea that would hurt students, and b) uni funding was tight, sure, but far from in crisis and certainly not unsustainable.[16]

But Pyne had hitherto enjoyed the support of the institutions with the nicest cloisters, and therefore had largely been able to argue that he was speaking for the sector. That all changed when the Go8 issued its statement on 31 March.

Sure, it admitted, fee deregulation would be lovely and everything. But, it conceded, 'the Senate has now twice voted

---

16 Just to be clear: Flinders University is a very, very tidy campus—despite, or possibly because of, the aforementioned ducks. Seriously, they run a tight ship.

down deregulation of fees while the funding crisis remains, and can only worsen with time. A solution therefore must be found if our students, and the nation, are not to suffer from the loss of quality this will create in both teaching and research. The Go8 is concerned that a number of other proposals being floated as solutions do not tackle the core issue of long-term funding satisfactorily.'

In other words: the Fixer had failed to do the necessary Fixing, and now it needed to get things fixed some other way.

16
WHO'S AFRAID OF HUMAN RIGHTS?

Or, 'Trigging in the Rigging'

When we last considered the state of asylum seekers under Australian law, things were . . . let's go with 'horrific'. You might remember people being killed, epidemic abuse, a culture of secrecy around the very operation of offshore detention centres and so on. It was only what, eleven chapters ago?

Things didn't change dramatically for the better after the Manus Island riots and the death of Reza Berati. Neither were they beneficially affected by the subsequent death on 9 September of Hamid Kehazaei, another Iranian asylum seeker on Manus Island, who cut his foot on the rocky ground of the camp—shoes being a rare luxury for detainees—and died in hospital when his heart gave out while being treated for the septicaemia that had set in.[1]

---

1   There is some disagreement about whether or not it was a result of neglect, poor medical care or horrible luck that Kehazaei's cut wasn't treated, but evidence from his family and other detainees indicated that authorities had refused to fly him to Brisbane for treatment until it was too late. Immigration minister Scott Morrison released a statement describing such suggestions as 'unhelpful and unfortunate'. Awwwww, *diddums!*

His death followed reports of outbreaks of tuberculosis and fungal infections among children in detention on Christmas Island, all of which put the centres' healthcare providers under an unwelcome spotlight.[2] The suggestion that Australia's detention centres were perhaps not achieving the sort of standards of hygiene and sterility as the cholera-filled trenches of World War I did not go over well with the government. Immigration minister Scott Morrison insisted that people were making assumptions about a situation 'not based on any primary knowledge of the event or the circumstances', which was correct—principally because he was assiduously preventing independent access to any information on the event and the circumstances.

One of the enduring problems that the government faced was the prickly issue of the 1951 Refugee Convention, which laid out in no uncertain terms the obligations to which all signatories were required to adhere. For example, the principle of non-refoulement (refoulement being the act of sending people back to countries from which they fled, while knowing that said people would face persecution).

There had been attempts to get around this by placing the burden of proof on the asylum seekers themselves as to whether they would be jailed and/or tortured if they were sent

---

2   In case there was any doubt as to the sort of care the asylum seekers were getting in detention, in July 2015 Sarah Hanson-Young referred International Health and Medical Services, the healthcare providers at both offshore and Australian detention centres, to the Australian Federal Police after *The Guardian* revealed that IHMS had failed to run background checks on employees, shared private detainee records with the Department of Immigration and Border Control, and deliberately falsified complaint reports to give the impression that incident reporting targets were being achieved, among other breaches.

back rather than, say, relying on knowledge the Australian government itself possessed.[3] Presumably this was an honest mistake on the part of the department, made under the erroneous assumption that, when people flee repressive regimes with few or no official travel papers, they are still somehow issued with an official document by their government confirming that they'll be punished upon their return.

But Morrison had an excellent plan, which he put into action in December 2014. It went a little bit like this:

He would authorise the transfer to Australia of the 108 children (and their family members) held in detention on Christmas Island in time for Christmas, as long as the Senate approved new fast-track application processing—or, more accurately, application refusal without appeal—plus the reintroduction of Temporary Protection Visas and the removal of all references to the Refugee Convention from Australian law. If senators did not pass the laws, then they would be held responsible for knowingly leaving children in an at-risk situation.

While the sensible response to this would have been to form a pitchfork-wielding mob and storm Morrison's castle stronghold, the Senate chose not to ask what sort of monster would hold the safety of children hostage in order to push through dubious legislation. It did, however, argue long into the night before six members of the crossbench chose to vote

---

3 Because, sure, the Rohingya people were being systematically persecuted by the Burmese government, but how was the Department of Immigration and Border Control supposed to know whether the authorities had particular plans for this *specific* Rohingya person? Eh, best just to send them all back, right? They'll probably be fine.

in favour of the immediate safety of kids at risk, despite their certain knowledge that these laws would lead to greater evil. And who could possibly blame them?

It was a political win for Morrison. Not an ethical one, obviously, but that was hardly the point any more.

———

Things were about to get even more horrific with the release of the Australian Human Rights Commission report, *The Forgotten Children*. The report stemmed from an inquiry into children in Australian detention, both onshore and on Christmas Island, and covered the period from January 2013 to September 2014—in other words, under both Labor and Coalition governments.

As the Australian Human Rights Commission's president, Gillian Triggs, made clear in her foreword to the report, 'The aim of the Inquiry was not to reconsider the Human Rights Commission's already formed legal views of immigration detention, but to investigate how the health, wellbeing and development of children was being affected by life in detention.'

It's not as though the government was under any illusions as to what the report would say. After all, in February 2014 then-immigration minister Scott Morrison banned Triggs from visiting Nauru, much less speaking to children in detention there. That's not, perhaps, the actions of a government determined to discover the truth.[4] Thus the report focused

---

4   The argument was that, since Nauru was a sovereign nation, the authority of the Australian Human Rights Commission didn't extend to its detention centres. The same applied to Manus Island, which is part of Papua New Guinea, and is why those two detention centres were not covered by the inquiry.

only on the experiences of children in detention in Australia and on Christmas Island. And it confirmed everything we already knew.

In the *Medical Journal of Australia* Triggs outlined the Commission's findings in a damning indictment of policy under the current and previous governments:

> The mandatory and prolonged immigration detention of children is in clear violation of the Convention on the Rights of the Child . . .
>
> Detention creates and compounds mental health problems in children.
>
> There are high rates of self-harm by children in detention.
>
> Children are detained in close confinement with adults who suffer high levels of mental illness.
>
> Children have been exposed to unacceptable levels of violence in detention.
>
> The harsh and cramped living conditions on Christmas Island created particular physical illnesses among children.
>
> The children detained indefinitely in Nauru are suffering from extreme levels of physical, emotional, psychological and developmental distress.
>
> Key recommendations of the report were:
>
> • That all children and their families in detention in Australia and Nauru be released as soon as possible.
> • That legislation be enacted so that children may only be detained for as long as is necessary for health, identity and security checks.
> • That no child be sent offshore for processing unless it is clear that their human rights will be respected.[5]

5   https://www.mja.com.au/journal/2015/202/11/forgotten-children-national-inquiry-children-immigration-detention-2014

It was all but assumed that the government would reject the findings of the report out of hand. After all, a similar approach had been taken by the Howard government in 1997, when *A Last Resort?*—a report looking at the conditions under which families and children were held in mandatory detention in Australia—was released. At that time the government had publicly pooh-poohed the report, with then-immigration minister Amanda Vanstone airily dismissing the findings as 'a part of history'. But clearly the Howard government took the findings seriously because it then, quietly but swiftly, started releasing families into the community.

The Abbott government got as far as the pooh-poohing, at least.

———

Gillian Triggs was aware that the document would be political, and did her best to defuse the issue in the foreword.

> By July 2013, the number of children detained reached 1992. As the federal election was imminent, I decided to await the outcome of the election, and any government changes in asylum seeker policy, before considering launching an Inquiry. By February this year [2014], it became apparent that there had been a slowing down of the release of children. Over the first six months of the new Coalition Government the numbers of children in detention remained relatively constant. Not only were over 1000 children held in detention by February 2014, but also they were being held for longer periods than in the past, with no pathway to resettlement.
>
> In these circumstances, I decided to exercise the Commission's powers under the Australian Human Rights Commission Act 1986 (Cth) to hold a National Inquiry into Children in Immigration Detention.

The PM wasn't going to take that sort of justified concern about the treatment of children in detention lying down.

Interestingly, neither was he going to dispute the findings of the report, which were not in any sort of doubt. No, he had a different plan in mind: shoot the messenger.

———

The government had known the contents of the report in late 2014 and in November Attorney-General George Brandis informed Triggs that, instead of releasing it, he'd very much like her to resign instead, thanks. However, the president declined the kind offer—although at that point no-one knew just how kind it was.

Public reaction to the release of the report was, predictably, explosive. But the government was ready to insist that, actually, it was all about saving lives at sea and the problem was that the HRC was insufferably biased against the government.

'I reckon that the Human Rights Commission ought to be sending a note of congratulations to Scott Morrison,' the PM hilariously declared in parliament on 12 February 2015, 'saying, "Well done, mate, because your actions have been very good for the human rights and the human flourishing of thousands of people."'

Who those thousands of human flourishing people were was not made clear, but fortunately Abbott would no longer need to rely on weird syntax to make his point: a drama-storm was brewing that would divert attention away from that messy children-being-abused business.

As questions were fired at her during a Senate Estimates meeting on 24 February, there was an extraordinary revelation from Triggs: that she had been encouraged to resign with the promise of a shiny new job—which, if true, would have been considered an inducement and be completely illegal. The person who supposedly made the offer was Chris Moraitis, departmental secretary of the attorney-general's office. According to Triggs, Moraitis had approached her with a request from George Brandis on 3 February. Said request was that she step down from her role as president of the Australian Human Rights Commission—a statutory role from which she could not be removed without proof of criminal misconduct. In return for her resignation with two and a half years still to run of her five-year role, Triggs claimed, Moraitis intimated that Brandis would make available another position—a senior role reflecting her expertise in international law.

'I rejected it out of hand,' Triggs said. 'I thought it was a disgraceful proposal.'

Brandis confirmed that, yep, he'd totally asked Triggs to resign and had 'lost confidence' in her.

Labor smelled blood in the water and immediately pounced. Had Brandis made an offer? Could the police investigate him for corrupt dealings?

Short answer: nope.

Brandis's statements regarding Triggs had been made in parliament and in Senate Estimates hearings, and were therefore covered by parliamentary privilege. For the Australian Federal Police to investigate at all, they would need some sort of other evidence. Like, for example, Moraitis's notes from the meeting, which he had confirmed he took.

Alas, Moraitis explained, the notes had been kept securely

in his briefcase, which—oh, what are the odds?—he then mysteriously lost. Oh, cruel fate!

'I had taken some notes of my discussion with the attorney and also annotated those notes after my discussion with Professor Triggs,' he explained on 24 February. 'I had those notes for a while and unfortunately I have travelled to three countries in two weeks and I have lost those notes, losing my briefcase by mistake. I am sorry.'[6]

While this sounded perfectly legitimate and not even a bit suspicious, Queensland barrister Alex McKean called bullshit and submitted a Freedom of Information request to the Attorney-General's Department, asking for details on the briefcase and on Moraitis's travel between September 2014 and February 2015.

His request was rejected on the grounds that it would be too much work, but the FOI person did add: 'To assist you to revise the scope of your request I can advise that the Secretary, Mr Moraitis, did not lose a briefcase during the period September 1, 2014, to February 28, 2015.'[7]

So . . . the briefcase *wasn't* lost? H-how could that be?

In any case, with no admissible evidence, the AFP was powerless to do anything, and the story withered on the vine.

Sensing victory, the Senate Estimates Committee's chair, LNP senator Ian Macdonald, joined the chorus, castigating Triggs for the partisan tone of the report—a claim that was undermined somewhat when he admitted that he hadn't actually so much as looked at it. Despite describing the report

---

6 'Also, a dog ate it.'

7 The *Saturday Paper* was responsible for this glorious little investigation (Richard Ackland, 'Gadfly: A case in point', 18 April 2015).

as 'not worth the paper it's printed on' and 'unnecessary, irrelevant and inaccurate', this grown man with a position of some responsibility said, with a straight face to a room full of adults, that he hadn't bothered to read the report because he'd decided 'not to waste my time on a report which was clearly partisan'.[8]

That pretty much summed up the government's approach: refusing even to discuss the report's findings while hysterically attacking the author in a desperate—and largely successful—attempt to deflect people's attention away from the issues. After all, looking like a bunch of crybabies is ethically preferable to looking like a government that knowingly permitted children under its protection to be raped and beaten.

———

The government knew that it had to look like it was doing something about children in detention even as it concentrated on Triggs's character assassination, and thus it commissioned its own independent review into the treatment of asylum seekers in detention.

Unfortunately the Moss Review, as it was called, not only confirmed everything that the Human Rights Commission had reported, but went further—thanks in no small part to its authors being able to investigate Nauru. They confirmed that abuse was rife there, that mental and physical health was poor, and that entire families—including children—were sleeping in un-air-conditioned vinyl tents, with little privacy and precious little safety. The Moss Review was released with little fanfare on 20 March, and reporting of its contents was

---

8 Seriously. Of all the wilfully stupid things said by a member of parliament in this book, that has to be the number-one most idiotic example, surely?

overshadowed by the tragic (but politically convenient) death of former prime minister Malcolm Fraser.[9]

But happily those sorts of negative stories were soon going to be a thing of the past as the government had a plan called the Border Force Act, which—among many other things— made it illegal for any workers in detention centres to report abuse, complete with a two-year jail sentence for doing so.

Teachers and doctors were especially outraged, pointing out that they're actually obliged under law to report any suspicion of child abuse and can be prosecuted for failing to do so.

Labor, having been given barely any time to read the legislation, supported it and thereby allowed it to pass in May, despite howls of protest from the Senate independents. Labor's immigration spokesperson, Richard Marles, responded to the criticism by insisting that legitimate whistleblowers would be protected under existing law—a claim which he may well have believed at the time but which was entirely false—not least because Australia's less-than-stellar whistleblower laws had no legal weight in Nauru or Papua New Guinea.

An open letter, signed by current and former detention centre staff, was published on 1 July, the day the Border Force Act came into effect. Over forty staff confirmed that they had witnessed abuse of children in detention; they demanded that the government remove all children from offshore detention and challenged the government to prosecute the signatories for speaking out.

At the time of writing, nothing had happened.

---

9   More than one commentator noted that Fraser—a long-time advocate for refugee and children's rights—would have been especially appalled by the report. In the words of William Shatner as Buck Murdoch in the justifiably underrated *Flying High II*: 'I guess irony can be pretty ironic sometimes.'

———

There were also mounting allegations that the companies contracted to run the centres were corrupt, inept, or both.

On 23 June, SBS released a secret video in which Greg Sheppard, a former director of Wilson Protective Services (a subsidiary of Wilson Security, the company contracted by the government to run the Manus Island detention centre), carefully explained how to bribe local officials to an actor purporting to be a fund manager looking to invest in Papua New Guinea. Sheppard, now working as a lawyer with Young and Williams in Port Moresby, didn't even bother to couch his advice in any sort of euphemisms as he and his partner, Harvey Maladina, explained on camera that the PNG government had to get its cut.

'It's something that needs to be handled very, very carefully,' Sheppard said. 'You've got to make sure it's not going to be attacked as money laundering . . . if you were to pay seven figures to anybody, the world would fall in on top of you . . . Small dribs and drabs are the only way to go . . . anyone who says seven figures, they are inviting prosecution.'

But the problem wasn't just the venality of PNG officials and of those bribing them; the current detention centre contractors were also not entirely living up to the highest of professional standards. On 20 July a Senate inquiry heard that sixty-seven allegations of child abuse had been made on Nauru—thirty against staff and thirty-seven against detainees—but exactly zero charges had been laid.

Transfield Services' commercial and strategy manager, Erin O'Sullivan, blithely told the inquiry that there had been some dismissals—although then director Angela Williams admitted that she couldn't be sure there had been any actual dismissals, but maybe some people had been switched to other duties—and twelve of the offences had been reported to police, but there'd been no arrests as far as she was aware. Transfield also confirmed that while it was supposed to test staff for drugs, it didn't actually do that because there were no drug-testing facilities.

Other highlights included a refusal by operations chief executive Kate Munnings to guarantee that Transfield could actually protect the detainees, and logistics manager Daron White admitting that ensuring those in camp had adequate water was 'challenging'. And, in a piece of particularly poor timing, on 27 July it was reported that three Australian guards had been sent home from Manus Island by the Department of Immigration and Border Control rather than face charges in Papua New Guinea for allegedly drugging and raping a local woman. Manus Island's local police were furious as they saw this action as a breach of their sovereign right to charge people for crimes on their own soil and, accurately, as a perversion of justice.

Inexplicably, however, none of these revelations seemed to shake the government or the Opposition's support for offshore detention as a border-control strategy. Not only did Labor confirm at its national conference in July that it would not reject turnbacks as policy,[10] but when a Vietnamese asylum seeker boat rather inconveniently turned up on the coast of

10 It's worth noting—because the government certainly did—that Labor didn't actually endorse turnbacks so much as refuse to rule them out (with the caveat 'when it is safe to do so', which is arguably 'never').

Western Australia and was discovered by civilians rather than members of the military, the public was forced to ask, 'Um . . . didn't the government say the boats had been stopped?'

Even the arrival of actual, physical boats didn't in any way dissuade advocates for the policy of offshore detention; both the Coalition and Labor sides of politics still insisted this was a necessary policy in order to stop the boats. That the boats had clearly not stopped, despite the fact that even reporting on the boats was now arguably illegal, didn't seem to alter either party's zeal for locking people up to (very literally) rot.[11]

Offshore detention appeared more and more to be the equivalent of discouraging housebreakers by surrounding one's home with a moat filled with human shit—even if the policy achieved the desired aims, clearly it was causing greater problems than it could hope to solve.

---

11 Starting with the teeth, if the Christmas Island experience was any indication.

17
THE HUNT FOR TEAM AUSTRALIA

In which the captain raises the flag. And another one.
And another one. And another one . . .

With the 2015 budget released, the Human Rights Commission cowed, leadership challenges thwarted and those uppity onions shown a thing or two, Abbott should have been riding high with the Australian public.

And yet . . . not so much.

While his public image had been rehabilitated to some degree, his habit of following up any PR win with a cringe-inducing gaffe meant that he really needed a good, unambiguous victory to finally cement the government in a position where it might hope to win another term. And so he turned to the one subject that had been a winner for every government since Fraser: border protection.

As discussed elsewhere, much of the rhetoric around (and

the lack of outrage regarding the treatment of) asylum seekers has been down to the conflation between 'desperate people asking for help, due to genuinely horrendous regional regimes' and 'our porous borders are putting us at risk'.[1] So what better way to emphasise the victory over Triggs and tap into the oh-so-Australian fear that someone's out to get us than by making a patriotic song and dance about keeping Australia safe? How to combine the fear of the outside world with the comforting sense of being 'straylian?

One word: citizenship.

————

In keeping with most of the Western world since 2001, mainstream Australia really wasn't above casting aspersions at its Muslim citizens—from attempts to outlaw headscarves and other traditional dress through to heated rhetoric about 'Australianness', in which it was all-but-implied that every Muslim was just a terrorist-in-waiting. And it wasn't a difficult argument to sell to the public either.

The Howard government had spun the Bali bombings of 2005 as confirmation that terrorism could strike Australia at any moment. And while that hadn't eventuated during the subsequent decade, the horrifying Lindt Cafe siege in Sydney's Martin Place in December 2014, during which two hostages were killed along with the gunman, did establish the notion of Islamic terror cells waiting to strike from within, rather

---

1   As Richard Cooke pointed out in *The Monthly* in July 2015, the Joint Standing Committee on Migration Regulations had identified this as far back as 1990, with its report that year including the telling quote: 'The presence of illegal entrants has come, whether correctly or not, to symbolise the inability of governments to control their borders.'

than the more accurate 'severely mentally ill man commits terrifying crime'.[2]

The revelations that the gunman was known to police and had not been considered a serious threat incensed the public, especially in Sydney. But, as luck would have it, the siege provided a convenient pretext for the passage of laws forcing mandatory data retention on internet service providers and telecommunications companies in Australia.

——

Up to now the government had been struggling to sell as a necessary security measure its proposed data retention laws, which had proven wildly unpopular, primarily because they were seen as an expensive and intrusive invasion of privacy, but also for the less well-known but possibly more important reason that they didn't work. While Australia was wrestling with whether to implement these supposedly vital new tools against the war on terror, in the US the FBI had concluded that more than a decade of data retention under the Patriot Act in the US had done nothing to keep Americans safe. Indeed, it concluded that data collection had proved crucial in only one case: that of San Diego taxi driver Basaaly Moalin, who was found to have donated $8500 to al-Shabaab, a Somalian group affiliated with al-Qaeda. While this was undeniably illegal, it was also clearly not an issue of national security. In June 2015, many of the data retention and surveillance

---

2   Man Haron Monis was a serial media pest and known provocateur with a shady criminal history, and authorities had flagged him as being unstable, although not necessarily violent. That's a whole book in itself, but the short version is that, despite efforts by the government in August 2015's inquest to suggest Monis had ties to terrorist groups the horrific events of 14–15 December had everything to do with Monis's mental state and was not part of any sort of coordinated Islamic State terror plot.

laws in the USA lapsed without any congressional effort to renew them.

Similarly Germany had introduced data retention laws during the aftermath of 9/11. They'd eventually been abolished on the grounds of being unconstitutional but, after looking at the statistics, a Bundestag working group provided a report showing that the overall crime clearance rate during the life of the laws (for all criminal activity, not just crimes affecting national security) had risen by 0.006 per cent.[3] In other words, the unwieldy and expensive legislation had resulted in a benefit that was indistinguishable from (and quite probably was) a statistical error.

However, these less-than-stellar outcomes overseas didn't in any way diminish the Abbott government's enthusiasm for the collection of metadata, a term so unclear that not even the attorney-general himself could explain what exactly it covered, much less how it would be used. This had been made clear in 2014 during a notorious disaster of an interview with David Speer on Sky News on 7 August, in which a stammering George Brandis explained metadata was like 'the name and address on an envelope' and failed to explain how retaining 'the address of a website' was somehow different to knowing what websites people were looking at.[4]

---

3   My year nine German is insufficient to read the original reports, but *PC World* provided a decent analysis (Jennifer Baker, 'Civil liberties groups slam EU data retention as unnecessary', *PC World*, 28 September 2011).

4   Incidentally, Brandis isn't the only government official unable to distinguish between a website URL and a site's IP address; in 2013 an ASIC attempt to block ten websites accidentally ended up putting over 250,000 sites on a government blacklist because it had confused the former with the latter. Do these people not have the internet?

In any case—despite concerns about the implementation, about the cost of retention,[5] about the fact that offshore companies like Gmail and Facebook were not covered (thereby putting Australian ISPs at a financial and legal disadvantage) and about the lack of any demonstrable necessity for the new laws—the PM took to the nation via his YouTube channel on 15 February 2015 to insist that he was sick of Australians being treated like 'mugs'.

'It's clear to me that for too long we have given those who might be a threat to our country the benefit of the doubt,' he declared in a powerful anti-mug statement. 'There's been the benefit of the doubt at our borders, the benefit of the doubt for residency, the benefit of the doubt for citizenship and the benefit of the doubt at Centrelink.[6] We are a free and fair nation. But that doesn't mean we should let bad people play us for mugs, and all too often they have. Well, that's going to stop.'

It was emphasised that these data retention laws would stop terrorism and child pornography, and absolutely weren't just a sop to the media companies lobbying government to do something about internet piracy.

No less an authority than the communications minister, Malcolm Turnbull, repeatedly emphasised that there were no plans to use the laws to go after individual media downloaders, although he generally did so while explaining various methods of getting around the mandatory data retention requirements,

5   Estimated by the Attorney-General's Office at an upper limit of $319.1 million, although data security experts pointed out that price didn't include any cybersecurity costs—which, when you're talking about a treasure trove of personal information, might be a wee bit necessary.
6   Yes, Centrelink. Heck, why *shouldn't* the prime minister cheekily imply that there's a link between unemployment and terrorism?

from the use of virtual private networks through to the adoption of various encryption apps he enthusiastically used.

The Telecommunications (Interception and Access)Amendment (Data Retention) Bill 2015 passed on 26 March and obliged service providers to store account holder details for two years, along with the date, time, duration and recipient of any communications, along with the location of said communications (such as mobile phone towers or wi-fi networks). The laws were immediately used to pursue internet piracy.

———

Those laws were a precursor to another dramatic piece of legislation for Australia's safety: the stripping of citizenship from those who travelled overseas to fight for the likes of Daesh in Syria and Iraq.

The initial proposal on which Abbott sought advice involved granting the government the power to remove Australian citizenship from individuals, even if they were citizens of no other country. This was determined to be legally dubious, since rendering a person stateless is frowned on in the international community. Indeed, statelessness is enough of a global problem for the United Nations to declare citizenship an essential human right.

Thus Abbott's desire to wash his hands of people he didn't like was curtailed—but the plan was amended. First, it was proposed to apply to people who technically could apply for citizenship elsewhere, but after accepting that that would be legally unworkable, it was limited to applying to dual citizens only.

The laws were also originally going to be deployed at the discretion of the immigration minister, who'd be able to strip citizenship from any suspect without any of that annoying oversight from the courts (or, indeed, necessity for clear evidence). But that was a step too far for Labor and the less hawkish elements in the Coalition, who may have had reasonable doubts about putting their complete trust in the unerring judgement of Peter Dutton.

While the PM made meaningful-sounding statements about how Australian citizenship was not 'a one-way street' and that 'those who come here must be as open and accepting of their adopted country, as we are of them', it wasn't clear how stripping people of citizenship would achieve greater openness and acceptance, much less multi-directional metaphorical roadways. In fact, the question of what problem this legislation was intended to solve seemed to go largely unanswered.

And it was an important question, because on the face of it the laws were, to all practical ends, pointless.

For a start, while the issue of Australian nationals joining Daesh was one worthy of concern, there wasn't exactly a flood of newly minted radicals flocking overseas. The total number of Australians who had gone overseas to fight numbered in the dozens, around half of whom were citizens of Australia only. Additionally, the sort of people travelling to fight in Syria and Iraq were explicitly doing so under the assumption that they'd be forging a new hardline Islamic nation or martyring themselves in the attempt, and therefore were probably not deeply concerned about being prevented from voting in the next Australian election or applying for a home loan. Removing their citizenship was, arguably, unlikely to prove a powerful deterrent.

Fortunately these sorts of inconvenient issues could be entirely ignored since the government was handed a PR godsend in the form of the ABC's *Q&A*. Specifically, by one member of the audience.

———

The government's relationship with the ABC generally and *Q&A* in particular had become increasingly fraught—because of the difficult-to-substantiate allegations of endemic left-wing bias in the case of the former, and the all-but-ubiquity of Malcolm Turnbull on the latter. Indeed, so frequently was the communications minister a panellist, it appeared that he was angling for a regular gig as co-host.

On 22 June 2015 the audience of *Q&A* contained one Zaky Mallah, a colourful figure who had been investigated (and acquitted) on terrorism-related charges, after being jailed for two years for threatening to kill ASIO officials. He'd seemingly mellowed somewhat since, even working with groups attempting to dissuade Muslim youth from becoming radicalised, and had also been in the *Q&A* audience before without incident.

Mallah submitted a question to be asked on the program, which was accepted. The question—which was directed to Liberal backbencher Steve Ciobo—was this:

'As the first man in Australia to be charged with terrorism under the harsh Liberal Howard government in 2003, I was subject to solitary confinement, a twenty-two-hour lockdown, dressed in most times in an orange overall and treated like a convicted terrorist while under the presumption of innocence. I had done and said some stupid things, including threatening to kidnap and kill, but in 2005 I was acquitted of those terrorism charges. What would have happened if my case had been decided by the minister himself and not the courts?'

Ciobo rose to the occasion: 'From memory, I thought you were acquitted on a technicality rather than it being on the basis of a substantial finding of fact. But I'm happy to look you straight in the eye and say that I'd be pleased to be part of a government that would say that you were out of the country as far as I'm concerned. I would sleep very soundly at night. I don't apologise for this point of view.'

Now, you may notice that this response didn't answer the important question of whether a government minister would have been in a position to deport a man on the basis of allegations for which a court subsequently found him to be not guilty. It was a deliberately provocative reply by an MP keen to make a point.

And it worked a treat, because a clearly fuming Mallah responded: 'The Liberals have just justified to many Australian Muslims in the community tonight to leave and go to Syria and join ISIL because of ministers like him.'

Now, in all fairness, Mallah was clearly badly mistaken in his statement; Ciobo is a backbencher, not a minister. But his larger point—that the government didn't seem to be terribly interested in discovering the truth when it came to situations concerning people about whom it had already made up its minds—was a pretty reasonable one. And that was completely lost in the resultant furore, which gave the government a chance to show it could be tough on border protection, citizenship and the ABC all in one hit.

It didn't muck around either. On 23 June the PM was in full grandstanding us-against-them mode, decrying the ABC as a 'leftie lynch mob' and piously declaring: 'I think many, many millions of Australians would feel betrayed by our national broadcaster right now, and I think that the ABC does have to have a long, hard look at itself, and to answer a question which I have posed before: whose side are you on?'

That same day he unveiled details of his revised proposal to amend the Australian Citizen Act. And if anyone missed the PM's endorsement of the sort of feel-don't-think jingoism that had once proved so successful for George W. Bush, he was flanked by a genuinely ridiculous backdrop of ten Australian flags.[7]

An investigation into *Q&A* was announced, followed by the PM banning any minister from appearing on the show—thereby forcing both Barnaby Joyce and a presumably disappointed Turnbull to cancel scheduled appearances. The patriotism or otherwise of the ABC was loudly discussed throughout the media and parliament, and the question about whether or not people had the right to challenge terrorism allegations against them in open court was conveniently shunted to one side.

Meanwhile the Australian Citizenship Amendment (Allegiance to Australia) Bill was barrelled through in the final sitting days of parliament by the government, again with Labor's support, with all sorts of prickly questions regarding oversight, what sort of evidence would be accepted and how the laws would be enforced remaining excitingly opaque.

---

7   *The Guardian's* Nick Evershed immediately created an interactive graphic of the PM's flag count per policy announcement in a hilarious yet genuinely instructive piece ('10-flag announcement brings government flag count to all-time high', 24 June).

18
EVERYWHERE WITH HELICOPTER

In which the captain faces an ecclesiastical conundrum:
can an Abbott punish a Bishop?

Parliament rose for the 2015 winter recess with the government looking united, fearless and strong—until something unfortunate came to light that ruined the recess for the captain and his crew and was to dominate the national media even more than Mallah's colourful appearance.

Coalition MPs had been expecting to spend some time in their electorates, maybe kick back with a relaxing drink and make the odd statement about how the unions were controlling Labor and the royal commission into union corruption left Bill Shorten with difficult questions to answer. What they didn't expect was to be quizzed over and over about helicopters.

Speaker of the House Bronwyn Bishop had, as mentioned earlier, been slotted into her role partly because the government correctly assumed she'd give them an easy ride in parliament and mercilessly punish the opposition for turning up. But this plum gig was also partly in recognition of her lifetime of service to the party—there was no way in hell that Abbott was going to appoint her to a ministerial position, but by this appointment he could avoid insulting such a venerable figure.

Bishop had done a lot over her time in parliament—starting in 1987 as a senator (making her the longest-serving woman in Australian federal parliament, incidentally) before moving to the House of Representatives in order to pursue her ambition to one day lead the party. The move to the lower house was achieved thanks to the resignation of Jim Carlton from the safe Liberal seat of Mackellar in Sydney's northern beaches, with Bishop easily winning the subsequent by-election. However, the closest she came to the leadership was opting out of a leadership challenge against John Hewson in 1994.[1] From there she was briefly shadow health minister, before being moved on after expressing her support for tobacco advertising. Her period as John Howard's Minister for Aged Care saw her badly mishandle a scandal when it was revealed that some private aged facilities were bathing their residents in kerosene solutions to combat scabies.

One thing at which she was remarkably adept over the years, however, was claiming travel allowances for her trips thither and yon. This propensity flared up every so often but, like most travel scandals, generally garnered a few 'our greedy entitled politicians' headlines and then calmed down. That's why she couldn't even be arsed apologising when it came to light on 15 July that she'd charged taxpayers for her travel

---

1 The winner—if that's the correct word—was Alexander Downer, who resigned eight months later after a gaffe-filled stint as Opposition leader and was replaced by the less-foolish John Howard.

expenses to a party fundraiser at the Clifton Springs Golf Club in November 2014 despite this clearly being a party event rather than an official duty. However, the outrage that ensued wasn't simply because she'd fiddled her entitlements. It was that the sum for reimbursement was an eye-catching $5227.27 for the trip from Melbourne to Geelong—which by car would be a drive of around an hour.

The reason it cost so much? She chose to go by helicopter.

The sheer gall of the claim caught the public imagination, leading to an outpouring of vitriol against Bishop in the media. What made it different to previous scandals was that this time around it didn't conveniently burn out in a few days but kept steadily growing in scope and intensity.

It didn't help that she'd recently charged the public purse $88,084 for a trip to Europe in a failed attempt to get the gig as president of the Inter-Parliamentary Union. Afghanistan beat her to the punch, but at least she had enjoyed some lovely taxpayer-funded accommodations, limousine travel, generous per diems and (naturally) business-class flights to take the sting out of her disappointment.

While she eventually agreed to pay the cost of her helicopter jaunt plus a $1307 penalty, she maintained that she still didn't need to apologise and that all her claims were perfectly above board.

At first her colleagues were largely supportive. Sure, Joe Hockey was caught off guard, agreeing with a conservative radio host that the claim didn't pass the 'sniff test', adding, 'I think Bronwyn Bishop should have the opportunity to explain exactly where the money went and what it was for.'

Bishop was unfazed, quipping, 'Joe says some funny things, doesn't he?'

However, backbenchers then started to talk about how the issue was hurting the party. Julie Bishop told Fairfax: 'I believe it's important the Department of Finance be able to carry out an investigation' into the claims. Parliamentary secretaries Kelly O'Dwyer and Paul Fletcher dodged questions when asked on Sky News whether they still supported the Speaker. And Malcolm Turnbull took the opportunity to live-tweet a train journey he just happened to be taking from Melbourne to Geelong, pointedly illustrating that his total journey had cost the taxpayer less than $12.

Bishop could have delivered a mea culpa at any time, but instead she instructed her office to deflect all enquiries with a blanket refusal to discuss the issue and a reiteration that she would not resign. It was left to Abbott to publicly insist that the Speaker was 'very contrite', which seemed . . . well, implausible.

Smelling blood in the water, the media pored over Bishop's travel claims and made discovery after discovery, including regular hiring of luxury cars (rarely mere taxis) to theatre premieres and opera events, and pricy hotels and plane flights to Albury and Brisbane on weekends that, as photos demonstrated, happily coincided with her attendance at the respective weddings of Liberal MPs Sophie Mirabella and Teresa Gambaro.

Other MPs had been caught using their travel entitlements to Mirabella's nuptials, including the PM himself, and had made a point of returning the money before the cries of 'rort!' got too loud. Bishop did not because, as she insisted, she was actually there in her capacity as chair of the Standing Committee for Family and Community Services, carrying out secret interviews for a report on work–life balance.

There were a couple of small problems with this, starting with the timing—it seems odd to conduct interviews over a weekend, especially one during which Bishop was confirmed to be at a wedding around forty-five minutes away in Wangaratta.[2]

There's also the *Balancing Work and Family* report itself, which was clearly based on material collected by submissions and public hearings, with no suggestion of data acquired during private meetings with anonymous people wanting to give clandestine insights into their work–life secrets.

Furthermore, according to the report, the committee held '25 public hearings between April 2005 and November 2006, taking evidence from over 200 witnesses in Sydney, Brisbane, Canberra, Hobart, Adelaide, Perth and Darwin'. You might notice that 'Albury' isn't on that list, nor any other Australian non-capital city.[3]

All this raised the possibility that the committee may not have, in fact, authorised this journey. However, as fellow committee member and Labor MP Kate Ellis helpfully pointed out, 'If there was a reason, if she did go through the proper processes, then there would be documentation and we wouldn't need to be here speculating about it. This is up to Tony Abbott and Bronwyn Bishop to put this matter to rest

---

2   It'd be quicker by helicopter, mind.
3   Also, why didn't Melbourne get a look-in? Were they too busy working to take part in the study?

and they should be able to do that very easily by just producing the documents.'

Oddly enough, no documents were forthcoming.

A similar situation arose around the trip to Gambaro's wedding. Bishop's office made the claim that the Speaker had a meeting with an unnamed academic with regards to the parliamentary inquiry into illicit drugs. Again, there should have been some sort of authorisation, which Bishop mysteriously failed to produce.

The cries for Bishop to step down grew stronger, not least because the Coalition, when previously in Opposition, had successfully prosecuted a campaign against the Speaker under Julia Gillard—former Liberal MP turned independent Peter Slipper—after it came to light that he'd claimed $900 in three Cabcharge vouchers. It was an eyebrow-raising sum, certainly, but considerably less than Bishop had spent on airfares to colleagues' weddings.

If there was a positive to be taken from the timing, it was that the controversy exploded during recess, rather than when parliament was in session. However, independent MP Andrew Wilkie indicated his intention to move a motion of no confidence in the Speaker and was supported in this by Clive Palmer, with Labor having every intention of doing the same. These motions couldn't pass, since the Coalition had control of the house, but, even so, this was an issue that needed to be either sorted out or buried deep by the time parliament resumed on 11 August.

On 30 July Bishop capitulated, after what was undoubtedly a great deal of backroom strong-arming: on Alan Jones's radio show she delivered a heartfelt non-apology, in which she reiterated that she had done absolutely nothing wrong and was under no obligation to pay back a cent of her travel entitlements, but would do because it 'just doesn't look right' to claim them.

On the same day as her radio appearance, *The Guardian* published a further fifteen travel claims lodged for committee chair business at times when either the committee was not holding hearings, or when there are no records of hearings being held in the city to which she travelled.

Two days later *The Daily Telegraph*—a newspaper which could be generally relied on to support the Coalition—revealed that Bishop had chartered a luxury aircraft (fixed-wing, this time around) in order to visit the New South Wales coastal centre of Nowra for a Liberal Party fundraiser in Berry. The cost to the taxpayer was $6000. She also made the confusing declaration to Jones that 'I won't be resigning, but I will be working very hard to make sure I mean my apology to the Australian people'.

How one works hard to mean an apology wasn't clear—but by that stage, neither was the future of the Speaker.

Through all of this turmoil Abbott stood resolutely by Bishop, insisting that she was apologetic about her actions and promising that there would be consequences, although it wasn't entirely clear what those consequences would—or, for that matter, could—be. If Bishop refused to resign, the only way to remove the Speaker was through a no-confidence motion in parliament, and it would hardly be a good look for the PM to move such a motion against the person he'd made such a show of elevating to the role in the first place.

Reports filtered through in early August that Bishop's planned trip to New York for an international meeting of parliamentary speakers had been quietly canned, but it wasn't immediately clear whether it was because she was having her travel curtailed or because the meeting was for current—rather than former—parliamentary speakers.

That was clarified on 2 August when Bishop fell on her sword, resigning as Speaker (though staying on as MP for Mackellar), with Abbott insisting that a) she was doing this as a noble and generous act by someone with a love for democracy, and definitely not because she was rorting the system to get the public to pay for her travel to weddings and free operas, and b) the prime minister was possibly in no hurry to prevent a recurrence of the furore by, say, tightening the rules around travel entitlements.[4]

During his press conference announcing Bishop's resignation, the prime minister stated: 'I think we should also be grateful that something has been done here that will resolve this vexed question of entitlements, as far is humanly possible, once and for all.'

A few hours later, *The Daily Telegraph* published a story revealing that deputy PM and Nationals leader Warren Truss had taken a private jet to a 'sod-turning' ceremony

---

4 As *The Guardian*'s Lenore Taylor determined in a lengthy piece before Bishop's announcement, claims around entitlements are largely at the discretion of the parliamentarian responsible and, surprisingly, there are no clear-cut rules about what can and cannot be claimed. Indeed, the laws are, in Taylor's words, 'so vague as to be unenforceable'. So essentially Bishop was correct in saying that she'd done nothing wrong; the only judge was Bishop's own conscience, and her conscience appeared to be pretty certain that she deserved everything she took ('Q: When are expenses legitimate', 31 July 2015).

in Port Macquarie, while other MPs flew via Qantas a few minutes later.

To be fair, asking Truss to fly commercial was, presumably, not humanly possible.

19
WHITHER LABOR?

In which we look at the ghost ship sailing behind the captain's vessel

Now, there's something that you might have noticed throughout this rollicking journey: the apparent absence of the Opposition.

Most of this book relies on facts—facts sieved through a snarky, cynical filter and vomited onto the page by an outspokenly partisan narrator, sure, but facts nonetheless. Yet, when it comes to contemplating the elevation of Bill Shorten to the position of leader of the federal Labor Party, there's a working theory that's hard to avoid.

It is this: when he was elected leader, Labor never expected him to lead the party to victory.

That's not a slight on Shorten, by the way. He had a solid history as a dedicated worker bee in the party—and, significantly, had enough political ambition to oversee the development of the National Disability Insurance Scheme, for which he was a tireless architect over many years, while stepping back to let his leader, Julia Gillard, take most of the credit when it was unveiled. That's the mark of a team player, and he had a good reputation as a problem-solver and a cross-factional solution-finder within the party.

What he undeniably was not, however, was an obviously inspirational leader. What's more, with a shadowy allegation of sexual assault in his past, the party must have known he was a risky proposition to take to the electorate.[1]

However, as Labor emerged exhausted, fractured and shell-shocked from the wreckage of the 2013 election, it needed someone who could reunite the party and start the difficult and challenging process of making the party competitive again. And Shorten—capable, likeable, can-do Shorten, the man who crossed the factional divide—was the obvious bloke for the job.

———

It seems that everyone (including the party's own strategists) was assuming that Labor was at least another term away from being a credible threat to the Coalition. After all, the one time a party had got only a single term in power in Australia was when the Labor government of Jim Scullin was turfed out of office in 1931—and it was defeated less by a powerful Opposition than by the Great Depression that inconveniently turned up two days after Scullin's swearing-in.

So it's entirely possible that those not entirely enamoured of Shorten would have been calculating that three years would

---

1   It should be noted that said allegations had been consistently denied by Shorten and the police found no case to answer.

provide time for Shorten to heal the party, take it to the 2016 election, lose with a reduced margin, and then—as Labor convention dictates—resign as leader and be replaced by a new, more invigorating figure who could return the party to government.

But then the government started making unforced errors and suddenly Labor was faced with an unexpected possibility: *Dear god, we could actually win the next election.*

The problem with making Shorten a plausible PM was compounded by a strange quirk that seems to infect the Labor Party machine, which is that whatever media management program it has in place to polish up a leader is evidently predicated on stripping away the fire and passion that got them the gig in the first place and presenting them to the public as creepily ingratiating and noncommittal.

Gillard is the best example of this: the outspoken and formidably intelligent firebrand was PRed into the nation's condescending, slow-talking auntie, making public statements that were in direct and obvious contradiction to things she'd previously said. This was most obvious with the subject of same-sex marriage, an issue about which she'd been a vocal supporter since her university days. But then she reversed her position, in a transparent attempt to woo voters—but the voters she was trying to woo were unlikely to line up behind an unmarried atheist woman PM in any case.

Even the worldwide public acclaim that followed Gillard's legendary 'misogyny speech'—when the cuddly *New Idea* pictorial image was ditched and the fierce, take-no-shit leader of the country emerged to tear into the Opposition leader—didn't apparently convince anyone in the party that having a leader who seemed to genuinely give a damn could be so crazy that it just might work.

With Shorten there appeared to be a half-hearted attempt to muss up his extant image as an earnest, hardworking backroom chap and to transform him into a slick-tongued political brawler in the Bob Hawke/Paul Keating mould.[2] That was, to be polite, a difficult sell: Shorten's inability to deliver a joke fast and credibly became part of his public image—especially once the ABC's satirical program *Shaun Micallef's Mad As Hell* began accompanying replays of Shorten's fumbling attempts to land a quip with a flashing 'ZINGER!' graphic and a lion's roar.

Frustratingly, there was a glimpse of the passionate street-fighting rabble-rouser in a video recorded in Sydney's Covent Garden Hotel on 5 July, the day before Shorten's first appearance at the Royal Commission into Trade Union Governance and Corruption. Looking a little unsteady on his pins, Shorten laid down the law in no uncertain terms: 'One day I hope that you belong in a country where marriage equality is legitimate, where our Aboriginal and Torres Strait Islander Australians are on the national birth certificate of the constitution, where people can organise to have a strong minimum wage,' he bellowed, before adding, '. . . and will not be subject to a royal commission!'

However, Shorten did not particularly distinguish himself after being dragged before the royal commission (aka the government's totally-unbiased-and-definitely-not-an-expensive-fishing-expedition-slash-witch-hunt). The allegation of a conflict of

---

2 Largely through getting him to stop wearing his glasses, it would appear.

interest during the former union secretary's negotiations with construction company Thiess John Holland—with whom the Australian Workers Union was nutting out a workplace agreement, while at the same time the company was making donations to the AWU—didn't capture the public imagination to the degree that the government had hoped. However, the linking of 'Shorten' and 'corruption' led to a massive hit to his approval rating.

Whatever pleasure that might have given the government was short-lived, though, since it did nothing positive for Abbott's fortunes: the PM's approval rating also dropped, and Labor remained ahead of the Coalition on a 52-to-48 per cent two-party-preferred basis—as it had been for most of the previous six months—and the entire Royal Commission descended into farce when it was revealed that the supposedly impartial commissioner, Justice Dyson Heydon, had accepted a speaking engagement at a forthcoming fundraiser for the NSW Liberal Party, and had also enjoyed a long connection with Tony Abbott, having been a member of the panel that awarded him the Rhodes Scholarship in 1980. The unions, not unreasonably, accused Heydon of clear political bias, and called for his resignation.

A bigger PR problem for Shorten was the screening of the Rudd–Gillard documentary series, *The Killing Season*, on the ABC in June. Not only did it remind the public of Labor's internal instability during what should have been its finest hour, it also painted Shorten in a very unflattering light, given that he was implicated in the coup against Rudd and then against Gillard.[3]

---

3   Although it could be argued that Albanese came across well—particularly in footage of him choking up when decrying the schism tearing Labor apart ahead of the first leadership spill.

More damagingly, the TV series claimed that one of Gillard's key supporters, NSW senator Mark Arbib, had specifically warned Gillard against making two ministerial appointments: that of Rudd to foreign minister, which kept him in the public eye and gave him a platform from which to damage Gillard, and Shorten to industrial relations, on the grounds that, in the words of Gillard's adviser Gerry Kitchener, 'You couldn't trust Bill Shorten, that he would do Julia in, that the one thing she couldn't do was ever give him Industrial Relations 'cause he'd use it to solidify the union base to knock her off.'

Given Shorten's original support for Gillard against Rudd and subsequent support for Rudd against Gillard, it was easy to paint him as serially disloyal—and the government didn't miss an opportunity to do exactly that.

'I want to say publicly thank you to the ABC. Thank you to the ABC,' Abbott declared on 17 June. 'I don't normally say thank you to the ABC, but I have to say Australia is indebted to you on this instance.'[4]

———

The criticism that was levelled at Shorten specifically and Labor generally at this time was straightforward: that neither was providing any sort of an alternative vision.

And this was true. Although, in Labor's defence, this was not merely practical—there was much rebuilding to be done, after all—but also almost certainly strategic. For a while there, Labor's strategy of not coughing up policies worked for a number of reasons.

---

4   This was before the Zaky Mallah *Q&A* leftie-lynch-mob kerfuffle, in case that all seemed oddly off-message for the PM.

First up, it was a party that needed to remember what it was about and what it wanted to present to the nation. A period of reflection and renewal was required, and while Labor was thus engaged the government very quickly became wrapped up in problems of its own making to scratch at Labor's wounds.

Second, if there's one thing that Labor learned to its considerable pain during the Gillard and Rudd eras, it was that Abbott was at his most formidable when he had a target to attack. Whenever he was in rabid attack-dog mode, his party locked into step behind him. By keeping schtum and providing a small target, Labor was depriving the government of its greatest strength—and giving the government the opportunity to busily bicker among itself.

And finally, why on earth would Labor want to distract the Coalition from making its numerous unforced errors?

However, a party that was even halfway together should have been able to put pressure on a government that had produced a suicide budget, had stumbled over its self-contradictions, and was in such disarray that the PM had been challenged by his own backbench. As time went on, this started to look less like a cunning plan and more like endless dithering.

As the 2015 ALP National Conference loomed, Labor either demonstrated admirable transparency with regard to the range of opinions it was willing to table on important subjects, or showed dangerous indecisiveness—depending on how sympathetic one wished to be. The conference offered a chance for the party to find its way again, committing itself to strong renewable energy targets (50 per cent renewable energy generation by 2030) and to a free vote on marriage equality[5]—the sort of things that could distinguish the party's strong points of difference from the Coalition under Abbott.

However, even at this moment the party was racked by division, when Shorten flagged his intention to make turning back boats at sea part of Labor policy—a move which the Left faction passionately opposed. Former speaker Anna Burke warned this would cost the party votes; Albanese declared that he had concerns about the policy and the way it was presented ahead of the party's decision, adding: 'I think that it is absolutely critical, critical that we always remember our need for compassion and to not appeal to the darker side.'

Shorten received boos when he announced his border protection plans,[6] even as other points in his speech—including the declaration that Australia should be a republic by 2025, as another symbolic point of difference from a government helmed by a fervent monarchist—received rapturous applause. And there's a reason why the party was grimly willing to skate over serious ideological divisions ahead of the coming general election: because, one way or another, at that point it had to believe that it could still possibly win with Shorten as

---

5   There was talk of a binding vote, most notably pushed by Shorten's deputy, Tanya Plibersek, whose not-unreasonable point was that bigotry and discrimination are not things that Labor should really um and ah about. The compromise was a free vote if the legislation comes before parliament this term, a free vote within a hundred days of Labor winning government under Shorten, and if things don't pass by then, a binding yes vote in Labor's second term. So . . . yay?

6   Yes, turnbacks are part of the deal (or, more accurately, not *not* part of the deal). But at least Shorten promised almost $450 million in funding to the UNHCR's regional programs, and also to reinstate the Refugee Convention to our border protection laws, after Scott Morrison merrily stripped it out of all relevant legislation. So . . . yay?

its leader. And if the conference achieved nothing else, it was confirming that the party was committed to putting its eggs into the basket marked 'Bill'. Mind you, like so much else in the party at that stage, it didn't have too many options on the table. Despite the likes of Albanese and (via their proxies) Plibersek and Senate leader Penny Wong voting against their leader on turnbacks, there was no suggestion of a viable leadership alternative–and, despite clear disagreement on the issue, the party still presented a united front.

However, as *The Killing Season* demonstrated, Shorten's loyalty has always been to one thing and one thing only: the Australian Labor Party. As Rudd and Gillard can (perhaps bitterly) attest, he's been prepared to put the objective best interests of the party ahead of his own personal desires when the need arises. It remains to be seen whether he chooses to apply the same clear-eyed expediency to his own leadership if (when?) the time comes.

And make no mistake, Shorten's going to have to change his tactics to defeat Turnbull in the Parliament. The new PM is less eager to rise to obvious bait than Abbott was, as well as less reliant on three-word sloganeering. The challenge for Shorten is to hold his own against the more rhetorically gifted new prime minister, which is no small task. If he can't manage that, he may well be facing his own awkward conversation with his deputy before the next election.

20
ABANDON SHIP!

In which the Captain succumbs to mutiny most foul!

At the end of August, as the government rounded upon its second anniversary in power, Tony Abbott spent his now traditional week in an Aboriginal community, this time in Cape York and the Torres Strait. There were numerous photos of the PM mucking in to hammer nails into school cubby houses but precious little suggestion of concrete policy.

By early September, the tone of the questions regarding Abbott's future had changed. Now there were fewer conversations about whether or not a leadership challenge would occur. The question now was 'when?' The Prime Minister had passed his self-imposed six month deadline to turn things around with no sign of any improvement in policy, popularity or polling—the Fairfax-Ipsos poll was predicting an eight per cent deficit to Labor, a trend confirmed by Newspoll.

Labor did not miss the opportunity to mark the occasion, with the member for Blaxland, Jason Clare, delivering a savage burn in Parliament on 9 September.

'It's a big day today,' he began. 'Today the Abbott government turns two, and what a terrific two years it has been. The deficit is up, debt's up, unemployment's up, taxes are up, the number of flags at press conferences is up. They've cut $50 billion from our hospitals, $30 billion from our schools, last year they tried to cut the pension . . . They've declared war on wind farms and the ABC, and they've even doubled the cost of their second-rate version of the NBN. This isn't the best of it. The Attorney-General George Brandis told us that people have a right to be bigots, the Treasurer told us that poor people don't drive cars, the Minister for Agriculture Barnaby Joyce threatened to kill Johnny Depp's dogs, Prince Philip got a knighthood, the Speaker got a helicopter and the Prime Minister ate an onion or two. What a cracking government we've got here!'

Admittedly, Clare delivered his sarcasm bomb on a Monday night to an almost entirely empty chamber, which may have lessened the impact at the time, but that comforting fact for Abbott was soon overshadowed by the 90 second clip going viral on YouTube.

Surprisingly, this came just before the brief, shining moment when it appeared that the government's position on refugees had softened, after the photograph of drowned three-year-old Syrian refugee Aylan Kurdi shocked the world into noticing the five-year civil war. Public demonstrations demanding immediate action to deal with the growing refugee crisis

sprang up around the country, and the PM made an unexpectedly swift humanitarian decision: that Australia would
accept 12,000 refugees from the region. However, even this
genuinely positive decision was tangled in gaffes and previous
mistakes and thus what could have been a brief moment of
national unity was much briefer and less unified than one
might have hoped.

No sooner had the announcement been made than Abbott
was struggling to convince the country that there was no
contradiction between this plan and Australia's current
detention policies, insisting that there was a 'world of difference' between the Syrian refugees who were languishing in
the camps in Turkey and Jordan, and the Syrian refugees
languishing on Nauru and Manus Island. There was further
confusion as various members of the government declared
that Christians would be given priority over Muslims, which
gave matters an unpleasantly bigoted sheen. Some hard-right
parliamentarians—most notably Cory Berndardi—openly
questioned the need to do anything at all.

But, most significantly, this moment of Abbott empathy was
accompanied by the announcement that Australia would join
the US in bombing missions over Syria, making the intake look
less like a humanitarian action and more like a way of justifying
Australia's military involvement. After all, it's tricky to argue
these people are selfish economic migrants determined to take
Australian jobs at the same time RAAF fighters were on the
way to the Middle East to actively bomb their villages.

While things were clearly going south for the government—and there was little hope of arresting the slide on the

horizon—it seemed unlikely that there would be a leadership challenge until closer to the end of the year, not least because an election would need to be called by March at the latest to avoid delivering what could be an unpopular pre-election budget. There also seemed little sense in a spill motion ahead of the 19 September by-election for the West Australian seat of Canning necessitated by the unexpected death of Don Randall.[1] After that Parliament wouldn't sit for another three weeks, making a spill all but impossible until it returned.

And maybe things would have been left in a holding pattern were it not for two troubling events.

———

On the same night Jason Clare was laying out the government's failings in House of Reps, Abbott was offering an unexpected olive branch to the lefty lynch mob at the ABC by appearing on *7.30* from Canberra before heading off to Port Moresby, where he was to attend the Pacific Island Forum. Host Leigh Sales asked Abbott about the humanitarian intake, why asylum seekers in detention would not be considered for release, and why Australia was contributing to the problem (giving Abbott another welcome opportunity to rail against the 'Daesh death cult'). That was all to be expected.

And then she asked about the economy. 'When Labor left office, unemployment was 5.8 per cent; it's now 6.3 per cent. Growth was 2.5 per cent; it's now two per cent. The Australian dollar was 92 cents; it's now around 70 cents. The budget deficit was $30 billion when you took office and now it's $48 billion.

---

1   Randall had supported the spill motion in February, so perhaps Abbott should have guessed it wouldn't save him now . . .

How do you explain to the Australian people that you were elected promising, in your words, to fix the budget emergency, yet in fact, Australia's economic position has worsened under your leadership?'

Abbott knew the talking points, and he was sticking to them. 'Well, I don't accept that,' he inauspiciously began. 'The boats have stopped. The carbon tax has . . .'

'We're talking about the economy,' Sales interrupted.

Abbott didn't miss a beat. 'The boats have stopped, the carbon tax has gone, the mining tax has gone.'

Multiple attempts by Sales to get back onto the question at hand were waved away as Abbott outlined his 'achievements'. When Sales disputed his claims about presiding over rising employment given that the unemployment rate was steadily increasing in the weakening economy, the PM's tone turned to admonishment that she should sully his rosy narrative with her base, negative facts.

'Leigh, I refuse to talk our country down,' he chided. 'I refuse to talk our country down and I hope the national broadcaster might join me in looking for the good and boosting our country, which has so much potential.'

Sales didn't blink. 'I wonder what you would've done if I'd helped Wayne Swan and Julia Gillard look for the good.'

———

While commentators and Twitter snarked about Abbott's all-purpose Stop The Boats response to unrelated questions, the PM was also drawing ire at the Pacific Island Forum.

As regional leaders gathered in Port Moresby, Abbott and New Zealand PM John Key patiently listened to the likes of

President Anote Tong of the tiny island nation of Kiribati talk about how rising sea levels and increasingly strong and frequent cyclones would force entire populations to flee. They responded by refusing to sign off on any increase in emission reduction targets or a target that would limit global temperature change to 1.5 degrees.

Abbott was castigated for the decision, but it was hardly a huge surprise: he'd made clear that Australia was not going to budge on the issue. The PM was feeling pretty content with his performance when, back in Canberra on Friday 11 September, together with Scott Morrison and Peter Dutton, he met with community groups about the Syrian refugee intake. These groups were taking a little longer than the trio would have wished, so they indulged in a bit of small talk as the media busied itself setting up cameras and, inconveniently, microphones—including a boom microphone that was just above Dutton's head.

'It's like Cape York time,' Dutton quipped to Abbott, in what sounded awfully like a dig at the punctuality of the communities they'd visited just over a week earlier.

'We had that a bit up in Port Moresby,' Abbott smirked in reply, all on camera. 'Anyway, it was a good meeting. It was a good meeting.'

And then Dutton lined up his zinger. 'Time doesn't mean anything when you're about to be, you know, have water lapping at your door.'

The PM brawed loudly at this *bon mot* and Dutton looked proud as proud could be—right up until Morrison leaned in and muttered, 'There's a boom there'.

And an expression passed across Dutton's face, almost as though he realised that he was about to star one of the fastest trending internet videos in Australia.

———

Within hours Dutton was avoiding questions on the subject from journalists, insisting that it was a 'private conversation' with the PM and that he had nothing more to say. Evidently this really was the media's fault for secretly recording him, rather than him saying something exquisitely foolish while very literally facing a bunch of cameras.

It was presently clear that this excuse wouldn't fly and by Sunday Dutton was offering a non-apology on Sky News, 'if anyone had taken offence to it'. 'It was a light-hearted discussion with the PM and I didn't mean any offence to anyone,' he defensively explained. 'If people have taken offence then they should accept my apology.'

Among those who very much took offence was Gerhardt Pearson, one of the traditional owners of Cape York, who didn't much care for the insinuation that his people were lazy. He described Dutton's language as filled with 'soft bigotry and low expectations', harking back to when 'white Superintendents ran our lives, dressed in their safari jackets and white helmets . . . and how they would look down at my hardworking grandfather, mother or brother, as though they were his slaves.'

Another was the exasperated Anote Tong, who was understandably irked by watching Australian politicians refuse to help address the terrifying consequences of rising sea levels one day and then see them making jokes about it the next.

'What kind of a person is he?' Tong rhetorically asked one journalist of Dutton. 'It shows a sense of moral irresponsibility quite unbecoming of leadership in any capacity.'

It looked like another in the long line of government missteps, but by this stage some hard decisions had been made.

A mutiny was coming. And this time, there would be a challenger.

———

Monday 14 September started like any other parliamentary sitting day, except that the PM was in Adelaide in an attempt to mollify an increasingly anti-Liberal electorate that it was a priority, despite the closure of the automotive industry and the back down on the submarine contracts. The gladhanding was particularly urgent, as new polling was showing that marginal Liberal seats were looking increasingly vulnerable to being snapped up by Nick Xenophon's party, NXT.[2] But the bigger threat to Abbott was about to come from within his own party.

By early afternoon he was back in Canberra for Question Time, which had been preceded by an unexpected conversation with his deputy Julie Bishop who told him that a leadership challenge was coming and that he no longer had the numbers to see it off. The meeting, according to Bishop later that week, did not go well.

When Question Time wrapped up just after 3 pm, Malcolm Turnbull bailed up the PM and they had a short meeting in which Abbott was reportedly offered an ultimatum: step down

———

2   Nick Xenophon Team. Presumably putting 'Excellent' in the middle to make the acronym 'NEXT' was seen as a step too far.

as leader, or face a challenge. Abbott, predictably, refused.

And thus, at 4 pm, Turnbull announced he was challenging Abbott for the leadership of the Liberal Party. And he didn't mince words either.

'Ultimately, the Prime Minister has not been capable of providing the economic leadership our nation needs,' he declared. 'He has not been capable of providing the economic confidence that business needs . . . We need a style of leadership that explains those challenges and opportunities . . . that respects the people's intelligence, that explains these complex issues and then sets out the course of action we believe we should take and makes a case for it. We need advocacy, not slogans.'

In case anyone in the party was still in any doubt about the situation, Turnbull baldly laid it out. 'The one thing that is clear about our current situation is the trajectory. We have lost 30 Newspolls in a row.[3] It is clear that the people have made up their mind about Mr Abbott's leadership . . . We have to make a change for our country's sake, for the government's sake, for the party's sake.'

Abbott returned service at 6.15 pm, declaring he would be a candidate in the spill ballot that very evening for both the leadership and deputy leadership of the party, 'and I expect to win'.

Looking more annoyed than scared, he continued. 'You can trust me to deliver a stronger economy and a safer community.

---

3   The choice of Newspoll was a deliberate signal to the party. Turnbull could have pointed out that the government was running behind Labor in every poll conducted for the best part of 18 months—Fairfax-Ipsos, Essential, Galaxy, ReachTel, Roy Morgan etcetera—but Newspoll's connection with News Corp presumably made it the only survey where the insidious influence of left-wing bias could be avoided, one assumes. That, or Turnbull only reads *The Australian*.

The prime ministership of this country is not a prize or a plaything to be demanded. It should be something which is earned by a vote of the Australian people.'

This was followed by a speech from Joe Hockey, which seemed less about reassuring the public that he supported the Prime Minister and more about making clear that if Abbott survived, he'd better not think of changing treasurers.

'Mr Turnbull made a number of claims about economic leadership that are completely unfounded. He has never said to me or to the Cabinet that we are heading in the wrong economic direction,' Hockey thundered. 'The disloyalty of some has been outrageous.'

That dig was directed not only at Turnbull, but at Julie Bishop as well—and any others thinking of backing the challenger. It was not known at the time whether Bishop had indicated to Abbott that he no longer had her support, nor that Christopher Pyne had also thrown his lot in with Turnbull. Scott Morrison, too, kept his mouth shut—although it was later discovered that he'd turned down the chance of standing as Abbott's deputy while indicating that he'd vote for the current leader in a clever bit of options-management. He was also, it seems, offered the Treasury portfolio by both sides, indicating that Hockey was out of luck regardless of the outcome.

Other members of the parliamentry party were not so demure about their loyalties, and rapidly slotted into two broad categories: the hopeful and the scared.

Turnbull supporters were backbenchers who knew their careers would be going nowhere under Abbott, including youthful Queensland MP Wyatt Roy and betrayed former assistant finance minister Arthur Sinodinos. Meanwhile, Abbott's staunchest supporters were mainly those who'd calculated they weren't going to keep their jobs on the basis of their performance. Dutton, Kevin Andrews and Eric Abetz immediately declared their allegiance to the PM, with Andrews even making an adorably optimistic play for the deputy leadership.

The party room went into lockdown at 9.15 pm, and the results were announced at 9.50 pm: Bishop had predictably won as deputy, but Turnbull had beaten Abbott 54 votes to 44.

And with that, after two-thirds of a term in office, Australia had its 29th prime minister.

———

The next twenty-four hours were not among Abbott's most triumphant, suggesting either a degree of deliberate and petulant heel-dragging or that he'd been genuinely blind-sided by losing a contest he had honestly assumed he'd comfortably win.

Turnbull and Bishop appeared at 11.10 that evening to deliver their victory speech, having given Abbott an opportunity to front the media first as per Hawke, Rudd and Gillard during their own leadership defeats—but the dethroned PM chose not to speak. This was to become something of a theme in the following days.

Abbott didn't come to Parliament House to address his colleagues on Tuesday morning, much less the joint party room meeting with the Nationals thereafter, amid rumours that his car had left the Australian Federal Police barracks where he stayed when in Canberra and was seemingly cruising the suburbs of Canberra.[4]

Parliament wasn't all that he was avoiding. It later came to light that he'd also neglected to visit the Governor General to offer his resignation, as per convention, and had instead sent Peter Cosgrove a fax. Anyone who has had to send an official legal document would know that fax is not an uncommon tool for transmitting important papers, but the sheer tech-adverse appropriateness of the act coming from the man who also downgraded the NBN was lost on few observers—not to mention the poetry of seeing the prime minister who endorsed coal-fired power, paternalistic policies for the unemployed and the continued denial of civil rights to gay Australians occupying his final minutes in the role using yet another tool long since superseded by superior alternatives.

While Turnbull prepared to be sworn in, Abbott's final act as PM was to deliver his concession speech. And, in his defence, it was at least representative of the man and his government: self-serving, filled with demonstrable falsehoods and quick to assign blame elsewhere.

'I've never leaked or backgrounded against anyone and I certainly won't start now,' he piously began. 'Our country deserves better than that.'

It was downhill from there, from a reeling off of dubious achievements ('The boats have stopped . . . and despite hysterical and unprincipled opposition, we've made $50 billion of repairs to the budget') and putting the blame for

---

4   Abbott's car was being followed and filmed driving around Manuka by a Sky News chopper, marking the second time in as many months that a helicopter had proved humiliating for the not yet formally defrocked PM.

his predicament on the exact same media that did so much of the heavy lifting for him in opposition. 'If there's one piece of advice I can give to the media, it's this—refuse to print self-serving claims that the person making them won't put his or her name to. Refuse to connive or dishonour by acting as the assassin's knife . . . We have more polls and more commentary than ever before, mostly sour, bitter, character assassination . . . and a febrile media culture has developed that rewards treachery.'

And with a round of applause from his staffers, he was gone. But there was one last thing.

While Abbott didn't appear in Parliament during the week, he did subsequently confirm that he wasn't planning to step down as member for Warringah, meaning that he'd be remaining on the backbench for the foreseeable future.

So perhaps the story of Captain Abbott hasn't ended *just* yet.

EPILOGUE
IS THIS THE BEST WE CAN DO?

In which we bid farewell to the captain . . . for now . . .

And so we leave the story of the Abbott Years, with its economic and policy hurdles, an embattled Opposition that was consistently ahead in the polls, and a front bench that was held together more through grim desperation than loyalty, as subsequent events proved.

As we've seen, the fortunes of both the Abbott government and Opposition were directed less by the steely wills of the party leaders than by the chaotic collisions of chance. Who'd have predicted that a plane being shot down on the other side of the world would have saved Abbott from awkward questions about the budget, or that the perfectly timed smear campaign against the Opposition leader would be inconveniently derailed by revelations that the Speaker of the House took a $5000 helicopter ride to a party function?

Barring some catastrophic war or act of terror, in 2013–15 the pendulum probably swung as violently to the right in Australia as it's likely to. One hopes that history will look back on the Abbott years as a time of some strange, selfish national delusion, when Australia inexplicably looked at the rest of the world doing it much, much harder and responded with 'But what about *me*?'

Assuming Malcolm Turnbull's government wants to stay in power, it's going to have to acknowledge some increasingly impossible-to-ignore realities: that climate change is real and already affecting Australia, that income inequality is a genuine risk to our stability, and that the desperate pursuit of budget surpluses impedes genuine and necessary progress. (In my heart of hearts I'd like this to be accompanied by 'Oh, and we can't afford to pretend asylum seekers are some sort of existential threat and so we're winding up mandatory offshore detention', but that would require both the major parties to admit to cruel, inhumane mistakes that they currently refuse to consider, much less acknowledge.[1] So, baby steps.)

———

Perhaps this is the moment to step back and ask: 'Is this really the best we can do?' And, despite what this book might imply, it's worth making clear that this is a bigger issue than the political personalities of the day.

It's easy to pretend that there was a golden era of Australian politics when we had *real leaders* and people were concerned about *nation-building* and *Australian values* and *forging a*

---

1 Although the thought of Morrison and Dutton sweating in the dock at the Hague as they're dragged over the coals about human rights violations has been a mighty comfort when writing the related chapters. *Goddamn*, that was hard going.

national identity and other meaningless phrases that are all but spoken in italics. Conservative Australian types get misty-eyed about the Robert Menzies epoch, while lefties canonise Gough Whitlam, and both are endlessly cited as periods when Australia was led by men of vision and principle, unlike the sorry specimens we have before us today.

And it's *arse*.

Politics in Australia—as in every country—has always and forever been a slippery dance conducted by manipulative snakes, utopian idealists, hardline ideologues and power-hungry careerists looking to exert power and/or line their pockets, mixed in with dedicated, principled people genuinely interested in making a positive contribution to their country. And right now, with Australia's two major political parties basically offering a choice between more of the same and a bit less of the same, the citizenry could be forgiven for thinking that these are the only choices on offer.

They're not. But it requires taking a little moment in order to get some perspective on what those other possibilities might be.

This is going to be a gear change compared with all the snark you've just read,[2] but indulge me for a moment. It's also going to require going back a bit—about 200,000 years, give or take—but there's a point to it, honest.

And that point is we need to help each other in order to survive. Not because it's good or it's right or it's smart—although all those things are true—but because humans are

---

2 And seriously: thank you for reading. That was a lot to slog through, I know. Who fancies a drink?

ridiculously vulnerable. We're naked and slow and easy to kill. We don't have shells or claws or mighty fangs. Evolution gave us plenty of reasons to die out aeons before you and I turned up. A baby foal is wandering around within an hour of birth. Don't try leaving a newborn baby in a field and seeing how quickly it copes. Seriously: don't.[3]

However, one thing we're really, *really* good at as a species is working together. We've had to be, because for a long time we were essentially conveniently portable high-protein sabretooth cat food.

A lot of species work together—but we've turned it into an art form (actually, hundreds of thousands of different art forms). We got so good at working together that we invented languages to express ever more intricate ways to work together. Along the way we started creating societies together and, as our societies became larger and more unwieldy, we developed systems to handle the necessary organisational aspects.

Out of that came governments. And surprisingly recently we discovered something great about governments: they could do things that were too complicated or too expensive or too multi-generational for individuals or private enterprises to achieve on their own, no matter how wealthy or motivated they were. Governments could develop and nourish great big expensive things that offered massive benefits to society but had few direct profit centres. Education systems. Healthcare. Sanitation networks. Police forces. Stuff like that. Stuff, in other words, that governments needed to do to preserve social

---

3   I can't stress that enough.

stability. Indeed, stuff that governments are uniquely well suited to doing.

And there's a reason why we work so well together. And, for want of a better word, it's . . . well, love.

One might rhapsodise about the mystery and majesty of that most glorious and noble of emotions, that unbreakable bond that links us, as if by ethereal thread, to those we hold dear. Or, alternatively, one might just be grateful for the cocktail of hormones and neurotransmitters that buzz around our brain's insula and striatum and make us care about each other enough to prevent the species going extinct. After all, they're the same thing.

For as long as vaguely human-shaped creatures have been walking upright, our bodies have been locked in an evolutionary battle between the size of skull required to hold our increasingly complicated (and thus ever-larger) brains and the size of skull that can descend through the human cervix. The compromise that evolution has hit upon is to plonk us out in a relatively undeveloped state. As mentioned above, the young of most other species can survive independently relatively quickly; humans don't, because by necessity we give birth to neonates that need long and constant care and attention if they're going to survive.[4]

For a long time survival favoured family units in which the mother cared for her child and her mate helped care for them both, and they lived among relatives who helped look after the kids, all the while keeping an eye out for sabre-toothed cats.

---

4   Really, do NOT leave babies alone in fields. I can't believe I even brought it up.

Thanks to natural selection, we became super-invested in one another—and that was hugely beneficial for a bunch of awkward, nomadic apes who, by all rights, should have been eaten to extinction by better-equipped species millennia before our distant African ancestors apparently went: 'Hey, let's all wander over that way and see if there's a route to what will one day be called Europe.'

The people who looked after each other flourished and reproduced. The people who could take or leave each other ended up as piles of bones quietly bleaching on the savannah.

Our mighty societies are testament to the fact that we do better together than alone. The societies that have endured longest have increasingly been the ones that balanced shared responsibility with personal freedom. Too much repression and people rebel; too little control and the people with the largest sticks eventually take over.

Over the last couple of centuries there seems to have been a positive correlation between the countries that were not being constantly rent asunder by civil and regional wars, and increasingly prosperous societies that found a stable-ish balance of control and freedom: enough law and order for people to feel reasonably secure that their children wouldn't be murdered, but enough freedom to do what seemed interesting with one's time on the planet. Even what eventually congealed as the nation of Australia, despite being created as one huge offshore detention centre with a sideline in cultural (and, in the case of Tasmania, literal) genocide, managed to make the transition.

That seems like a pretty fine balance to strike.

And that's why I think governments are a great idea: they do all the stuff that keeps a society stable. And a stable society—such as Australia's—is a good place to live: not in an abstract All Support Team Australia way, but because stability has tangible, measurable benefits.

People live longer. They prosper. They live more fulfilling lives. And by contributing some of our common wealth in the form of tax, some of our common time in the form of democracy, and some of our common loudmouths in the form of our elected representatives, we all benefit.

Sure, no-one likes doing their tax returns. Every small business owner will merrily talk one's ear off about red tape and onerous bureaucratic requirements, but at least they don't have to spend valuable trading time hacking out paths to their office door through the unrelenting jungle, or defending their business from raids by vicious marauding bands. Chipping in a bit to maintain the existence of society is a sweet bargain.

And that lies at the core of what I think should be the fundamental question for any government, and for any policy of any government: *Does this make things better for people?*

There are always going to be plenty of questions to discuss about priorities, costs versus benefits, methodology and so on—and good people can honestly disagree. However, when you start from that basic question, it makes those calculations a lot more clear. It's harder to hide behind slogans and value statements when you need to justify how closing a hospital or jailing asylum seekers is unambiguously making lives better— and that's especially true when people dare to point out that there's a fundamental difference between an economy and a society.

And those are the sort of questions that our politicians aren't getting asked so much these days. Maybe we should be doing that.

———

Of course, who has the time to ask those sorts of existential questions about human happiness? There's going to be an election to be won!

And there's going to be another one in Australia really, really soon,[5] which is quite possibly why you picked up this book.

Assuming that you made it to this point, it's reasonable—indeed, sane—to feel disheartened about the state of the country right now; that is, if you're the sort of person who likes other people and thinks we should look after each other a bit more. Disgust and cynicism is a perfectly valid response, especially after everything you've just slogged through.[6]

However . . . here's something to remember.

All progress happens in exciting little bursts, followed by long, stagnant periods when things are unnecessarily difficult. We're in one of those now. The captain becalmed us—but there's a sense that the wind might be rising again.

Australia is a small, rich, educated nation—especially compared with others in our region. We are at peace—a perhaps increasingly strained one, sure—with our neighbours. We are capable of doing so very, very much with our wealth and our smarts—for our country and for the rest of the world. We've

———

5   If it hasn't happened already. Goddamn, writing a book while history is actually happening makes perspective difficult.
6   Seriously: thank you.

done it before. And—whisper it quietly—we're actually *really, really good at it*. Historically, Australia has punched well above its weight in everything from literature to sport to astronomy to human rights to portraying Marvel superheroes.[7]

Our reputation's taken a hit in recent times, sure, but we can turn it around. To make the point again: we've done it before.

Wouldn't it be kind of awesome to live in a country internationally respected for being a haven of democracy and human rights, with a passion for science and technology, and a genuine conscience about the basic wellbeing of everyone within (and beyond) its borders?

It hardly seems unrealistically utopian—hell, we were doing some of that stuff in the 1950s. And the 1960s. And the 1970s and 80s, for that matter. If anything, this should be even *more* achievable now.

If there's one thing that I honestly hope becomes the legacy of Captain Abbott, it's showing Australians that we're better working together than splintering into political ghettoes and economic pressure groups. We have seen what happens when we fight among ourselves and seen how quickly stuff falls apart. Maybe it's time to start playing to our strengths again.

People right now care a hell of a lot more about their government than they have throughout any other era of Australian history that I can remember—and an engaged,

---

7 Don't take my word for it: Hugh Jackman's Wolverine and Chris Hemsworth as Thor, obviously, but also Luke Mitchell was Inhuman in *Agents of S.H.I.E.L.D.* and Julian McMahon was Dr Doom in the second terrible *Fantastic Four* film, and two of the child actors in the *X-Men Origins: Wolverine* film were Australian (Michael-James Olsen and Troye Sivan). Oh, and Rachel Taylor and Eka Darville were both cast in the *A.K.A. Jessica Jones* pilot. I'm not proud that I know this stuff either.

active electorate is a positive thing, especially since we have compulsory voting.[8]

Maybe—just maybe—going through the small-minded, scared, angry, petty Abbott era is the antidote we needed to combat the slow poison of decades of public apathy about politics.

And just think about what that would mean if we actually pulled it off: fifty-odd years after Horne's wry backhander, we could *genuinely* be the lucky country.

See you there, team.

---

8 Still the single best idea we've ever had. To any non-Australian reading this and contemplating building their own representative democracy based on the Westminster system, might I recommend that you too go with compulsory voting? It obliges everyone to at least pay a modicum of attention to what's going on in their country. Oh, and there are also often terrific sausage sizzles.

ACKNOWLEDGEMENTS
OR WHO'S TO BLAME
FOR THIS BOOK

Look, I never meant to write about politics.

That I do at all is largely the fault of Marcus Teague, then deputy editor at TheVine.com.au, who invited me to take over the site's 10 Things column in 2012 and didn't bat an eyelid as it stopped being about wacky internet memes and instead became largely a snarky rant about the state of Australian politics.

So this is effectively his fault, really, and also the fault of Alyx Gorman, Jenna Clarke, Anna Horan and Jake Cleland, who oversaw editorial matters at various points during my tenure. And of *Time Out* Sydney, especially Nick Dent, who let me drift from music and comedy into my growing obsession with parliament.

Fairfax and *The Sydney Morning Herald* is even more responsible since they then gave me the 'View from the Street' column and allowed me to rant regularly to the entire nation. Thank you Judith Whelan, Conal Hanna, Georgia Waters and the industrious night editors and social media team who get the thing out there five evenings a week.

My editors at Allen & Unwin are the most to blame of all, though, for inviting me to write a book in the first place. The charming and erudite Richard Walsh is a champion of a human being—not least for talking me into this and then talking me down after realising for what I'd very literally signed up. The unflappable and kind Rebecca Kaiser guided this thing from manuscript to print and answered a lot of very stupid questions along the way, and comprehensive thanks are due to copy editor Ali Lavau, who fixed my typos and accurately pointed out that there are certain words I really do use a lot. Like, a *lot*.

Thanks are also due to two of my former *Time Out* colleagues: Daniel Boud, who shot the misleadingly handsome author photo of me, and Robert Polmar, who did the awesome cover. Gentlemen both.

I owe a lot of people a lot of drinks for either giving advice, reading bits of this thing as it rapidly congealed, or just telling me that it was all going to be OK. Particular thanks to Marc Fennell, who talked me into taking the meeting about this in the first place and gave excellent advice when I accurately said 'sure, but I have no idea how to write a book'.

Thanks to my sprawling and multitudinous family for their love, support and intuitive sense of when to ask 'so, how's the book going?' and when to change the subject.

Thanks also to the many cafes of Sydney's inner west, where I discovered that the stereotype of the jerk with a MacBook, slamming coffee and tapping away for hours at a time, was entirely and tragically accurate.

Most of all, thanks are due to the impossibly patient Dee Street, who was Dee Hurley at the beginning of the process and still inexplicably went through with a wedding that occurred weeks after I agreed to write this, well before she knew what she was getting into.

As best as I can tell she's the very finest person on the planet and I'm impossibly fortunate to have her in my life-corner.